Beef

BLOOMSBURY KITCHEN LIBRARY

Beef

Bloomsbury Books
London

This edition published 1995 by Bloomsbury Books,
an imprint of The Godfrey Cave Group,
42 Bloomsbury Street, London, WC1B 3QJ.

ISBN 1 85471 518 6

Printed and bound in Great Britain.

Contents

Grilled Fillet Steaks with Roasted Garlic Sauce

Serves 4

Working time: about 30 minutes

Total time: about 50 minutes

Calories 170

Protein 20g

Cholesterol 55mg

Total fat 6g

Saturated fat 2g

Sodium 100mg

4	fillet steaks (125 g/4 oz each)	**4**
2	whole garlic bulbs, cloves separated but not peeled	**2**
½ tsp	juniper berries, crushed	**½ tsp**
1 tsp	cracked peppercorns	**1 tsp**
¼ litre	red wine	**8 fl oz**
3	shallots, sliced, or ½ small onion, finely chopped	**3**
½ litre	unsalted brown or chicken stock	**16 fl oz**

Preheat the oven to 240°C (475°F or Mark 9).

Scatter the garlic cloves in a small baking dish and roast them until they are very soft—20 to 30 minutes. Set the garlic cloves aside to cool.

If you plan to barbecue the steaks, light the charcoal about 30 minutes before cooking time; to grill, preheat the grill for about 10 minutes.

In a small bowl, mix together the juniper berries and pepper. Press the mixture into both sides of each of the steaks and set them aside at room temperature.

Pour the wine into a small, non-reactive saucepan and add the shallots or onion. Boil the mixture over medium-high heat until nearly all the liquid has evaporated—about 5 minutes. Add the stock, bring the liquid to the boil, and continue cooking it until it is reduced to about ¼ litre (8 fl oz)—about 5 minutes.

Squeeze the garlic pulp from the skins into a food processor or a blender. Pour in the stock and purée the garlic. Put the garlic sauce (it will be thick) into the saucepan, and keep it warm.

Cook the steaks for approximately 3 minutes on each side for medium-rare meat. Serve the steaks with the garlic sauce.

South Seas Kebabs

Serves 4

Working time:
about 35
minutes

Total time:
about 2 hours
and 30
minutes
(includes
marinating)

Calories
180
Protein
19g
Cholesterol
45mg
Total fat
4g
Saturated fat
2g
Sodium
195mg

500 g	rump steak, trimmed and cut into 2 cm (¾ inch) cubes	**1 lb**	**1**	spring onion, thinly sliced	**1**	
1	ripe papaya, peeled, seeded and cut into 2.5 cm (1 inch) cubes	**1**	**2**	garlic cloves, finely chopped	**2**	
1	sweet red or green pepper, deribbed, cubed	**1**	**2 tbsp**	finely chopped fresh ginger root	**2 tbsp**	
	Honey-ginger glaze		**1 tbsp**	honey	**1 tbsp**	
17.5 cl	unsalted brown or chicken stock	**6 fl oz**	**¼ tsp**	salt	**¼ tsp**	
			¼ tsp	cracked black peppercorns	**¼ tsp**	
			1 tbsp	cornflour mixed with 1 tbsp water	**1 tbsp**	

Purée one third of the papaya in a food processor; set the remaining cubes aside. Mix the beef and the papaya purée in a shallow dish; cover the dish and marinate the beef in the refrigerator for about 2 hours.

For the glaze, combine the stock, spring onion, garlic, ginger, honey, salt and peppercorns in a small saucepan over medium heat. Bring the mixture to a simmer and cook it for 3 to 4 minutes. Stir in the cornflour mixture and continue cooking and stirring the glaze until it thickens—1 to 2

minutes. Remove the glaze from the heat and set it aside. To assemble the kebabs, thread the cubes of beef, papaya and pepper on to four 30 cm (12 inch) skewers.

On a pre-heated grill, cook the kebabs for 3 minutes. Turn them and cook them for 3 minutes more. Brush with glaze and cook them for 1 minute. Turn the kebabs once more, brush them with the glaze, and cook them for another minute. Transfer the kebabs to a platter and brush them with the remaining glaze; serve immediately.

Marinated Beef Salad with Potatoes and French Beans

Serves 4

Working time: about 25 minutes

Total time: about 3 hours (includes marinating)

Calories
295
Protein
29g
Cholesterol
75mg
Total fat
11g
Saturated fat
3g
Sodium
150mg

600 g	sirloin steak, trimmed, 2.5cm (1 inch) thick,	**1¼ lb**
1	small onion, thinly sliced	**1**
1	garlic clove, finely chopped	**1**
½	sweet green pepper,	**½**
⅛ tsp	cracked black peppercorns	**⅛ tsp**
1 tbsp	chopped fresh tarragon, or 1 tsp dried tarragon	**1 tbsp**
2	lemons, juice only	**2**
250 g	waxy potatoes, scrubbed and cut into cubes	**8 oz**
350 g	French beans, trimmed	**12 oz**
⅛ tsp	salt	**⅛ tsp**
1	ripe tomato, cut into wedges	**1**
4 tsp	safflower oil	**4 tsp**
1 tsp	Dijon mustard	**1 tsp**

Mix the onion, garlic, green pepper, peppercorns and tarragon. Scatter half in a shallow dish. Put in the steak and sprinkle the rest of the mixture on top. Add the lemon juice and let marinate for 2 hours at room temperature.

Boil the potatoes until they are tender,—7 to 10 minutes, drain and let cool. Set a steamer in the pan with 2.5 cm (1 inch) water and bring to the boil. Add the beans, cover and steam until they are just tender—about 5 minutes. Refresh and drain the beans and put them into a large salad bowl.

Preheat the grill. Remove the steak from

the marinade and pour the marinade into a saucepan. Bring to the boil and cook for 2 minutes. Set aside.

Pat the steak dry, season it and grill for 4 minutes each side for medium-rare. Rest it for 30 minutes then cut into thin strips, 5 cm (2 inch)

Let the steak rest at room temperature for 30 minutes, then slice it into thin strips, 5 cm (2 inch) long. Mix it with vegetables.

Strain the marinade into a bowl. Whisk in the oil and mustard to make a vinaigrette. Pour over the salad and toss well. Refrigerate for 20 minutes before serving.

Sirloin and Leek Kebabs

Serves 4

Working (and total) time: about 1 hour

Calories 335
Protein 28g
Cholesterol 75mg
Total fat 7g
Saturated fat 3g
Sodium 210mg

600 g	sirloin steak, trimmed and cut into 1 cm (½ inch) strips	**1¼ lb**	
½ tsp	ground white pepper	**½ tsp**	
1 tsp	cayenne pepper	**1 tsp**	
½ tsp	ground allspice	**½ tsp**	
½ tsp	ground cumin	**½ tsp**	
½ tsp	turmeric	**½ tsp**	
¼ tsp	salt	**¼ tsp**	
3	leeks, white parts cut into strips,	3	

Ginger chutney

75 g	sultanas	**2½ oz**
5 cm	fresh ginger root, peeled and chopped	**2 inch**
½	small onion, chopped	**½**
1	tart apple, cored and quartered	**1**
12.5 cl	fresh lime juice	**4 fl oz**
1 tbsp	honey	**1 tbsp**
¼ tsp	whole mustard seeds	**¼ tsp**

To make the chutney, chop the sultanas, ginger, onion, apple, lime juice, honey and mustard seeds in a food processor or a blender. Transfer to a bowl and refrigerate it.

If you plan to barbecue the kebabs, light the charcoal about 30 minutes before cooking time; to grill, preheat for about 10 minutes.

Combine the white pepper, cayenne pepper, allspice, cumin, turmeric and salt in a small bowl. Spread the strips of beef on a baking sheet or tray. With your fingers, rub the spice mixture into the beef. Set the beef aside.

Blanch the leeks in a large saucepan of boiling water for 2 minutes Drain them and refresh them under cold running water, then drain them again.

Lay a strip of leek on top of each piece of meat. Divide the meat and leeks among 12 skewers, threading the skewer through both leek and meat at frequent intervals.

Barbecue or grill the kebabs for 1 minute on each side for medium-rare meat, and serve them with the ginger chutney.

Tournedos with Pepper Sauces

Serves 4

Working time: about 1 hour

Total time: about 2 hours 15 minutes (includes marinating)

Calories 280
Protein 26g
Cholesterol 75mg
Total fat 12g
Saturated fat 4g
Sodium 190mg

600 g	beef fillet, trimmed of fat and cut into eight small steaks	**1¼ lb**
1	garlic clove, finely chopped	**1**
¼ litre	red wine	**½ pint**
30 g	fresh rosemary sprigs, or 1½ tbsp dried rosemary	**1 oz**
3	sweet yellow or green peppers	**3**
3	sweet red peppers	**3**
2 tsp	red wine vinegar	**2 tsp**
¼ tsp	salt	**¼ tsp**
1	large aubergine, sliced into eight rounds	**1**
1 tbsp	olive oil	**1 tbsp**
8	fresh rosemary sprigs	**8**

Put the steaks into a shallow dish and sprinkle on the garlic, wine and rosemary. Marinate at room temperature for 2 hours.

After 1 hour grill the peppers until their skins blister. Transfer to a bowl and cover with plastic film to loosen the skins. When the peppers are cool, peel, seed and derib them over a sieve set in a bowl to catch the juices. Cut one of the yellow or green peppers and one of the red peppers into small dice.

Purée the remaining two yellow or green peppers. Add 1 teaspoon of the vinegar, ⅛ teaspoon of salt and half of the pepper juices and pour into a small saucepan. Purée the re-maining red peppers and add the remaining vinegar, salt and pepper juices, and pour into a small saucepan. Warm both sauces gently.

Score both sides of each aubergine slice in a crosshatch pattern. Lightly brush both sides with the oil, then grill until they are soft and browned. Remove from the grill and keep warm.

Remove the steaks from the marinade and pat them dry. Grill until they are medium-rare—about 3 minutes per side.

Place two aubergine slices on each plate. Set a steak on each slice and spoon the sauces round the steaks. Garnish with the diced peppers and fresh rosemary.

Fillet Steaks Stuffed with Oysters and Topped with Kale

Serves 6

Working
(and total)
time: about
1 hour

Calories
185
Protein
23g
Cholesterol
75mg
Total fat
6g
Saturated fat
2g
Sodium
195mg

6	fillet steaks, trimmed (about 125 g/4 oz each)	**6**
12	shucked oysters, with their liquid	**12**
6	shallots, finely chopped	**6**
3 tbsp	white wine vinegar or red wine vinegar	**3 tbsp**
4 tbsp	unsalted brown or chicken stock	**4 tbsp**
250 g	kale, coarsely shredded	**8 oz**
¼ tsp	salt	**¼ tsp**
	freshly ground black pepper	

If barbecueing the steaks, light the charcoal about 30 minutes before cooking time; to grill, preheat the grill for about 10 minutes.

Poach the oysters in their liquid in a saucepan over medium heat just until their edges curl—about 1 minute. With a slotted spoon, remove the oysters from the pan and set them aside. Strain the poaching liquid and reserve it.

Cut a slit in the side of each steak to make a pocket large enough to hold one of the oysters. Stuff the steaks with six of the oysters.

Cook the steaks on the barbecue or under the grill for 2 to 3 minutes on each side for medium-rare steaks. Set the steaks aside in a warm place.

Heat the shallots, vinegar and stock in a large heavy frying pan over medium-high heat until the liquid boils.

Continue cooking the mixture until it has reduced by one third—3 to 4 minutes. Stir in the kale, the remaining oysters, the poaching liquid, the salt and some pepper. Toss the mixture until the greens begin to wilt—about 2 minutes.

Spoon the kale and oysters over the steaks and serve immediately.

Veal Chops Dijonnaise

Serves 4

Working time:
about 15
minutes

Total time:
about 2 hours
30 minutes
(includes
marinating)

Calories
255
Protein
23g
Cholesterol
120mg
Total fat
16g
Saturated fat
5g
Sodium
120mg

4	veal chops, each weighing 175 to 200 g (6 to 7 oz), trimmed	4
3 tbsp	capers, drained and crushed	3 tbsp
2 tbsp	virgin olive oil	2 tbsp
2 tbsp	fresh lemon juice	2 tbsp

2 tsp	Dijon mustard	2 tsp
2 tsp	chopped fresh tarragon, or 1 tsp dried tarragon	2 tsp
	freshly ground black pepper	
	fresh tarragon sprigs (optional)	

Place the four veal chops side by side in a shallow dish. Put the capers, oil, lemon juice, mustard, chopped tarragon and some pepper in a jug and whisk them together. Brush the mixture over both sides of the chops.

Cover the dish and leave to marinate in a cold place for 2 hours.

Preheat the grill. Place the chops on the grill rack and grill for 10 minutes, basting frequently with the marinade. Turn the chops over and grill for another 10 minutes, again basting them with the marinade. Pour over the cooking juices from the grill pan and garnish with the tarragon sprigs, if using. Serve hot.

Paupiettes of Veal in Avgolemono Sauce

Serves 4

Working
(and total)
time: about
1 hour

Calories
285
Protein
28g
Cholesterol
135mg
Total fat
11g
Saturated fat
3g
Sodium
355mg

4	veal escalopes, each weighing 90 to 125 g (3 to 4 oz), trimmed	4
3	small red onions, quartered	3
1 tbsp	virgin olive oil	1 tbsp
	freshly ground black pepper	
	Anchovy stuffing	
6	canned anchovy fillets, soaked in 6 tbsp of milk for 20 minutes, drained, rinsed and patted dry	6
150 g	fresh granary breadcrumbs	5 oz

1	lemon, grated rind only	1
2 tbsp	lemon juice	2 tbsp
4 tsp	chopped fresh chervil or parsley (or mixture of the two)	4 tsp
	freshly ground black pepper	
	Avgolemono sauce	
30 cl	unsalted chicken stock	½ pint
1	egg yolk	1
1	lemon, juice only	1
1 tsp	arrowroot	1 tsp
	freshly ground black pepper	

Cut each escalope into four equal pieces, Then coarsely chop the anchovy fillets and put them in a bowl. Add the breadcrumbs, lemon rind and juice, chervil or parsley and some pepper. Preheat the grill. Spoon one sixteenth of the stuffing on to each piece of veal.

Roll the veal up neatly round the stuffing, then squeeze the paupiettes so that they hold together. Thread four on to each of four metal skewers, alternating with onion quarters. Place on the grill rack, brush with half the oil and

sprinkle with some pepper. Grill for 2 to 3 minutes. Turn, brush with oil, sprinkle with pepper and grill for a further 2 to 3 minutes.

For the sauce, put the stock in a saucepan and bring to the boil. Remove from the heat. Mix together the egg yolk, lemon juice and arrowroot. Add a little of the hot stock, then add this to the stock in the pan. Simmer, whisking, until the sauce thickens. Add pepper to taste. Pour some sauce on to individual plates and arrange the paupiettes and onions on top.

Veal and Mushroom Burgers with Mango-Pineapple Relish

Serves 4

**Working time:
about 50
minutes**

**Total time:
about 1 hour
and 35
minutes**

**Calories
325
Protein
22g
Cholesterol
70mg
Total fat
9g
Saturated fat
3g
Sodium
370mg**

350 g	topside of veal or top rump, trimmed of fat and finely chopped	12 oz
175 g	chestnut mushrooms, finely chopped	6 oz
30 g	shelled walnuts, chopped	1 oz
½ tsp	salt	½ tsp
	freshly ground black pepper	
⅛ to ¼ tsp	cayenne pepper	⅛ to ¼ tsp
1	egg white	1
2	wholemeal muffins, halved	2
	watercress or shredded lettuce	

Mango-pineapple relish

1	small unripe mango (about 250 g/8 oz), peeled, stoned and finely diced	1
250 g	fresh pineapple, diced	8 oz
1	small onion, finely chopped	1
1½ tsp	freshly grated ginger root	1½ tsp
1	small cinnamon stick	1
4	cloves	4
1	bayleaf	1
1	lime, grated rind and juice	1
½ tsp	Chinese chili sauce	½ tsp

Put the diced mango and pineapple into a saucepan and add the onion, spices, bay leaf, lime rind and juice. Cover and cook for about 45 minutes, stirring occasionally, until the fruit is tender. Add a little water as necessary. Discard the cinnamon stick, cloves and bay leaf. Stir in the chili sauce and let cool.

Put the veal, mushrooms and walnuts in a bowl, add the salt, some pepper and the cayenne pepper, and mix by hand, adding enough egg white to bind. Divide into four portions and shape each into burgers about 1 cm (⅜inch) thick. Place on a plate, cover and chill for 20 minutes.

Preheat the grill. Grill the burgers for 8 to 10 minutes on each side or until cooked and browned. Just before the burgers are ready, toast the muffins on both sides. Cover the muffin halves with watercress or shredded lettuce and place a burger on top. Serve with the relish.

Veal and Aubergine Kebabs with Strawberry and Cucumber Sauce

Serves 4

Working time:
about 1 hour

Total time:
about 1 hour
and 40
minutes

Calories
200

Protein
25g

Cholesterol
75mg

Total fat
5g

Saturated fat
2g

Sodium
295mg

175 g	veal topside or top rump, trimmed of fat and minced	**6 oz**
1	small aubergine (about 175 g/6 oz), peeled and chopped	**1**
¼ tsp	salt	**¼ tsp**
1	large sweet red pepper	**1**
1	garlic clove, chopped	**1**
175 g	chicken breast meat, minced freshly ground black pepper	**6 oz**
½	lemon, grated rind only	**½**

2 tbsp	chopped fresh mint	**2 tbsp**
1 tbsp	chopped parsley	**1 tbsp**
60 to 90 g	fresh bread crumbs	**2 to 3 oz**
8	large black olives, stoned	**8**
Strawberry and cucumber sauce		
125 g	cucumber	**4 oz**
15 cl	plain low-fat yogurt	**¼ pint**
45 g	strawberries, hulled and finely chopped	**1½ oz**
2 tbsp	finely sliced fresh mint	**2 tbsp**

Put the aubergine in a colander, sprinkle over 1 teaspoon of the salt and weight down with a plate. Leave to drain for 20 minutes. Meanwhile, grate the cucumber, then wrap it in paper towels and squeeze out excess moisture. Mix with the yogurt, strawberries and mint. Cover and chill.

Grill the pepper until the skin becomes blistered then place in a bowl, cover with plastic film and leave to cool. Peel and seed the pepper, and cut it into 2.5 cm (1 inch) squares.

To make the kebabs, rinse the aubergine

and squeeze it dry in your hands. Blend it in a food processor with the garlic. Transfer the purée to a bowl and add the veal, chicken, remaining salt, some black pepper, the lemon rind, mint and parsley. Mix well together by hand, then work in enough breadcrumbs to firm the mixture. Shape into walnut-size balls and chill for 30 minutes.

Preheat the grill. Thread the meatballs, red pepper and olives on to skewers. Grill, turning, for 15 to 20 minutes. Serve with the strawberry and cucumber sauce.

Oaty Veal Escalopes Viennese-Style

Serves 4

Working
(and total)
time: about
45 minutes

Calories
255
Protein
22g
Cholesterol
90mg
Total fat
12g
Saturated fat
2g
Sodium
210mg

4	veal escalopes	**4**
	(about 90 g/3 oz each)	
	trimmed and flattened	
30 g	flour	**1 oz**
¼ tsp	salt	**¼ tsp**
	freshly ground black pepper	
1	egg white	**1**
60 g	fine oatmeal	**2 oz**
2 tbsp	safflower oil	**2 tbsp**
	lemon wedges for garnish	

Put the flour, salt and pepper on a large plate or sheet of greaseproof paper, mix together and spread out evenly. Lightly beat the egg white with 1 tablespoon of water in a small bowl. Spread out the oatmeal on another plate or sheet of greaseproof paper.

Dip one escalope in the seasoned flour to coat both sides, and shake off excess flour. Place the escalope on a flat surface and lightly brush and dab the egg white over one side. Turn the escalope over, and place on the plate of oatmeal, egg side down. Press down gently. Brush and dab the top side of the escalope with egg white, turn it over and press gently into the oatmeal. Cover any still exposed areas of escalope with oatmeal so that it is evenly coated, pressing it on gently with your fingertips. Shake off excess oatmeal. Coat the remaining escalopes in the same way.

Heat 1 tablespoon of the oil in a large, heavy frying pan over medium heat. Add two of the escalopes and cook for 7 to 10 minutes in all, turning to brown evenly. When cooked, transfer the escalopes to a warm platter and cook the remaining escalopes in the same way.

Garnish with the lemon wedges and serve.

Beef Fillet and Potato Roast

Serves 4

Working time:
about 20
minutes

Total time:
about 1 hour
10 minutes

Calories
290

Protein
27g

Cholesterol
75mg

Total fat
9g

Saturated fat
3g

Sodium
145mg

600 g	beef fillet trimmed of fat and cut into eight slices	**1¼ lb**
½ tsp	ground allspice	**½ tsp**
4 tbsp	chopped parsley	**4 tbsp**
1 tbsp	red wine vinegar	**1 tbsp**
⅛ tsp	salt	**⅛ tsp**
500 g	potatoes, scrubbed and cut into 5 mm (¼ inch) thick slices	**1 lb**
2	onions, thinly sliced	**2**
12.5 cl	unsalted brown or chicken stock	**4 fl oz**

Preheat the oven to 180°C (350°F or Mark 4).

Mix the allspice, 2 tablespoons of the parsley, the vinegar and the salt in a small bowl. With your fingers, rub this mixture into the beef pieces and place them in a shallow dish. Let the meat marinate at room temperature while you make the potato gratin.

Combine the potatoes and onions in a fireproof baking dish. Pour in the stock and ¼ litre (8 fl oz) of water. Bring the liquid to the boil over medium-high heat, then bake the potatoes in the oven until they are tender and have browned—about 45 minutes. (If you do not have a fireproof baking dish, bring the potatoes, onions, stock and water to the boil in a saucepan, then transfer the mixture to a baking dish, and proceed as above.)

When the potatoes are cooked, remove the dish from the oven and increase the temperature to 230°C (450°F or Mark 8).

Heat a non-stick frying pan over medium-high heat. Pat the beef slices dry with a paper towel and sear them for 30 seconds on each side. Set the beef on top of the potatoes and return the dish to the oven. Bake the beef and potatoes for 3 minutes; turn the meat and bake it for 3 minutes more.

Sprinkle the remaining 2 tablespoons of parsley over the top before serving the roast.

Layered Meat Loaf

Serves 8

Working time:
about 40
minutes

Total time:
about 2 hours

Calories
220

Protein
23g

Cholesterol
55mg

Total fat
8g

Saturated fat
3g

Sodium
230mg

850 g	beef topside, minced	1¾lb	1 tbsp	sugar	1 tbsp
500 g	ripe tomatoes, skinned, seeded and chopped	1 lb	¼ tsp	salt	¼ tsp
1	onion, chopped	1		freshly ground black pepper	
3	garlic cloves, finely chopped	3	6 tbsp	freshly grated Parmesan	6 tbsp
1½ tsp	chopped fresh oregano, or ½ tsp dried oregano	1½ tsp	60 g	dry breadcrumbs	2 oz
			1	egg white	1
12.5 cl	port or Madeira	4 fl oz	1 tbsp	safflower oil	1 tbsp
2 tbsp	red wine vinegar	2 tbsp	2	bunches watercress,	2
			1 tbsp	fresh thyme, or 1 tsp dried	1 tbsp

Place the tomatoes, onion, garlic and oregano in a large pan and cook, stirring occasionally, for 5 minutes. Add the port, vinegar, sugar, ⅛ teaspoon of the salt and some pepper. Cook until most of the liquid has evaporated. Purée and place all but 4 tablespoons in a bowl. Preheat the oven to 200°C (400°F or Mark 6).

Add the beef, cheese, half the breadcrumbs, salt, some pepper and the egg white to the tomato mixture. Mix well and set aside.

Heat the oil in a large, heavy frying pan over high heat. Add the watercress, thyme and some pepper. Cook, stirring, until the

watercress has wilted and most of the liquid has evaporated—3 to 4 minutes. Chop the watercress. Mix with remaining breadcrumbs.

Divide the beef mixture into three. Flatten each portion into a rectangle 2 cm (⅔ inch) thick. Place one in a shallow baking pan. Spread on half of the watercress mixture. Lay another rectangle on top and cover it with the remaining watercress. Add the final rectangle, then spread the reserved tomato sauce over all. Sprinkle on the remaining Parmesan and bake for 1 hour and 10 minutes. Let the meat loaf stand for 10 minutes before serving.

Roast Beef with Root Vegetables

Serves 8

Working time: about 20 minutes

Total time: about 2 hours

Calories 205

Protein 24g

Cholesterol 60mg

Total fat 7g

Saturated fat 2g

Sodium 165mg

1-1.1kg	rolled beef topside or top rump, trimmed of fat	**2¼ lb**
1 tsp	safflower oil	**1 tsp**
¼ tsp	salt	**¼ tsp**
½ tsp	cracked black peppercorns	**½ tsp**
1	garlic clove, finely chopped	**1**
250 g	small white onions	**8 oz**
2	large carrots, peeled and sliced into cm (¾ inch) rounds	**2**
2	large turnips, peeled and cut into 1 cm (½ inch) wedges	**2**
1	swede, peeled and cut into 2 cm (¾ inch) cubes	**1**
½ tbsp	fresh thyme or ¾ tsp dried thyme	**½ tbsp**
4 tsp	cornflour	**4 tsp**
4 tbsp	semi-skimmed milk	**4 tbsp**
2 tsp	grainy mustard	**2 tsp**

Preheat the oven to 170°C (325°F or Mark 3).

Heat a large frying pan over medium heat. Add the oil and sear the roast in the pan for about 1 minute on each side. Transfer the meat to a roasting pan, sprinkle with the salt, peppercorns and garlic, and roast until it is medium rare and registers 60°C (140°F) on a meat thermometer—about 1¼ hours.

Remove from the pan and set aside. Skim fat from the juices in the pan and set this aside.

Toss vegetables with the thyme. Pour enough water into a large pan to fill it 2.5 cm (1 inch) deep. Place a vegetable steamer in the pan and bring the water to the boil. Add the vegetables to the steamer, cover the pan, and cook until they are tender—about 10 minutes.

Pour about ¼ litre (8 fl oz) of the steaming liquid into the roasting pan. Simmer the liquid over medium heat, stirring constantly. Mix the cornflour and milk in a small bowl, then whisk into the pan. Stir until the sauce thickens, then whisk in the mustard. Remove the pan from the heat and keep it warm.

Slice the roast and arrange on a platter, with the vegetables tossed in some of the sauce. Serve the remaining sauce separately.

Spicy Beef Salad

Serves 4

Working time: about 25 minutes

Total time: about 2 hours 45 minutes (includes marinating)

Calories 295
Protein 22g
Cholesterol 55mg
Total fat 5g
Saturated fat 2g
Sodium 120mg

500 g	sirloin steak in one piece, trimmed of fat	**1 lb**
8	whole cloves	**8**
8	black peppercorns	**8**
12	allspice berries	**12**
1	large onion, thinly sliced	**1**
2 tbsp	brandy	**2 tbsp**
½ litre	red wine	**16 fl oz**

175 g	mixed dried fruit, coarsely chopped	**6 oz**
4 tbsp	red wine vinegar	**4 tbsp**
1	cinnamon stick	**1**
500 g	turnips, peeled, halved lengthwise and sliced	**1 lb**
4 tbsp	chopped parsley	**4 tbsp**
	watercress sprigs (optional)	

Marinate the steak in a shallow pan with the cloves, peppercorns, allspice berries, onion slices, brandy and ¼ litre (8 fl oz) of the wine for two hours. In a saucepan, combine the dried fruit with the vinegar, the remaining wine, ¼ litre (8 fl oz) of water and the cinnamon stick. Bring to the boil, then simmer for 30 minutes. Drain the fruit in a sieve set over a bowl, discard the cinnamon stick and set the fruit aside. Return the liquid to the saucepan and boil for about 5 minutes to reduce by half.

Preheat the oven to 240°C (475°F or Mark 9). Pour 2.5 cm (1 inch) water into a saucepan.

Set a vegetable steamer in the pan and bring the water to the boil. Add the turnips, cover the pan, and steam until tender—about 10 minutes. Transfer them to a bowl and set them aside.

Remove the steak from the marinade and pat it dry; discard the marinade. Roast the steak for 15 minutes, then remove it from the oven, and let it rest for 30 minutes. Cut against the grain into thin slices. Cut each slice into strips about 4 cm (1½ inches) long.

Toss the beef with the reduced wine mixture, parsley, turnips and the reserved fruit. Arrange on a platter; garnished with watercress, if you wish, and serve.

Skewered Meatballs with Aubergine Relish

Serves 8

Working time:
about 1 hour

Total time:
about 1 hour
30 minutes

Calories
235
Protein
26g
Cholesterol
60mg
Total fat
7g
Saturated fat
2g
Sodium
190mg

1.1 kg	beef topside, trimmed of fat and minced	**2¼ lb**
1 kg	aubergines, pierced in several places with a knife	**2 lb**
2	onions, finely chopped	**2**
6	garlic cloves, finely chopped	**6**
1 tsp	olive oil	**1 tsp**
3 tbsp	fresh lemon juice	**3 tbsp**
4 tbsp	chopped fresh mint, or 2 tsp dried oregano	**4 tbsp**
¼ tsp	salt freshly ground black pepper	**¼ tsp**
4	slices wholemeal bread	**4**
5 tbsp	chopped parsley	**5 tbsp**
12.5 cl	plain low-fat yogurt several mint sprigs (optional)	**4 fl oz**

Preheat the oven to 240°C (475°C or Mark 9).

Roast the aubergines, turning them, until blistered on all sides—about 20 minutes. Transfer to a bowl, cover and refrigerate.

Simmer the onion, garlic, oil and 4 tbsps water in a heavy saucepan until the onion is translucent—about 5 minutes. Increase the heat and boil until the water has evaporated.

For the relish, peel the aubergines and purée the flesh in a blender. Remove 4 tbsps and set it aside. In a small bowl, combine the rest of the aubergine with the chopped mint or dried oregano, lemon juice, half of the onion and garlic mixture, ⅛ tsp of the salt and

plenty of pepper. Put the aubergine relish into the refrigerator.

Soak the bread slices for 3 minutes in water, then squeeze the water from the bread.

Mix the beef, bread, parsley, the rest of the onion and garlic mixture, the reserved purée, the remaining salt and plenty black pepper. Form the mixture into 48 meatballs. Thread three on each of 16 skewers and place them on a baking sheet. Cook in the oven until browned—10 to 15 minutes.

Arrange the meatballs on a platter and garnish with sprigs of mint. Serve the relish and yogurt separately.

Mediterranean Meat Loaf

Serves 10

Working time:
about 1 hour

Total time:
about 2 hours

Calories
220
Protein
22g
Cholesterol
50mg
Total fat
6g
Saturated fat
2g
Sodium
140mg

1-1.1 kg	beef topside, trimmed of fat and minced	2¼ lb	8	garlic cloves, finely chopped	8
1 tsp	olive oil	1 tsp	6	large ripe tomatoes, skinned, seeded and chopped, or 800 g (28 oz) canned whole tomatoes, crushed and drained	6
1	small onion, peeled and grated	1			
2	sticks celery, finely chopped	2			
2	onions, finely chopped	2	4 tbsp	finely chopped fresh oregano, or 4 tsp dried oregano	4 tbsp
500 g	aubergine, finely chopped	1 lb			
1	sweet red pepper, seeded, deribbed and finely chopped	1	135 g	fresh bread crumbs	4½ oz
			2 tbsp	currants (optional)	2 tbsp
1	sweet green pepper, seeded, deribbed and finely chopped	1	20	vine leaves (optional), stemmed, rinsed and dried	20

Cook the carrots, celery, onions, aubergine, peppers and garlic in the oil, stirring frequently, until soft—about 8 minutes. Add the tomatoes and oregano, increase the heat, then simmer for 2 minutes. Remove half the mixture and set it aside. Cook the mixture remaining in the pan until the liquid has evaporated—about 10 minutes. Put the vegetables in a bowl and let them cool slightly. Add the beef, the breadcrumbs and the currants and knead well.

Preheat the oven to 180°C (350°F or Mark 4).

Line a 3 litre (5 pint) ring mould with the vine leaves if you are using them. Spoon the meat mixture into the mould, patting it down to release trapped air.

Bake the loaf for 1 hour. After about 50 minutes, reheat the reserved vegetable mixture over medium heat. Invert a serving plate on top of the mould; turn both over, then gently lift off the mould. Fill the space in the centre of the meat loaf with some of the hot vegetables and spoon the rest into a bowl.

Roast Fillet of Beef with Spinach Sauce and Almonds

Serves 6

Working
time: about
20 minutes

Total time:
about 1
hour

Calories
230
Protein
22g
Cholesterol
65mg
Total fat
13g
Saturated fat
3g
Sodium
165mg

850 g	beef fillet in one piece, trimmed of fat	**1¾ lb**
4 tsp	safflower oil	**4 tsp**
¼ tsp	salt	**¼ tsp**
	freshly ground black pepper	
2 tbsp	slivered almonds	**2 tbsp**

3 tbsp	finely chopped shallot	**3 tbsp**
¼ litre	dry white wine	**8 fl oz**
250 g	fresh spinach, stemmed and washed	**8 oz**
4 tbsp	skimmed milk	**4 tbsp**
⅛ tsp	grated nutmeg	**⅛ tsp**

Preheat the oven to 170°C (325°F or Mark 3).

Heat 1 teaspoon of the oil in a large frying pan. Sear the meat in the pan until it is browned on all sides—2 to 3 minutes. Season the fillet with ⅛ tsp of the salt and plenty pepper. Transfer the fillet to a roasting pan; do not wash the frying pan. Finish cooking the meat in the oven—about 35 minutes, or until a thermometer inserted in the centre registers 60°C (140°F) for medium-rare meat.

Heat a small frying pan over medium heat. Add the slivered almonds and toast them, stirring, until lightly browned—2 to 3 minutes. Remove from the pan and set them aside.

For the sauce, heat the remaining oil in the large frying pan over medium heat. Add the shallot and cook it until it is translucent—about 2 minutes. Pour in the wine and simmer the liquid until about 6 tablespoons remain—6 to 8 minutes. Remove the fillet from the oven while you complete the sauce.

Add the spinach to the mixture and lower the heat. Cover the pan and cook the spinach until it has wilted—1 to 2 minutes. Stir in the milk and nutmeg. Return the mixture to a simmer, then use a blender to purée it. Season with the remaining salt and some pepper.

Carve the beef into 12 slices and arrange them on a warmed serving platter. Spoon some of the sauce over the slices and sprinkle them with the almonds. Serve the remaining sauce separately.

Roast Sirloin with Mushroom Sauce

Serves 10

Working time: about 30 minutes

Total time: about 1 hour

Calories 205
Protein 21g
Cholesterol 55mg
Total fat 10g
Saturated fat 3g
Sodium 170mg

1.25 kg	boned and rolled sirloin, trimmed of fat	**2½ lb**
4 tbsp	cracked black peppercorns	**4 tbsp**
2½ tbsp	Dijon mustard	**2½ tbsp**
2 tbsp	plain low-fat yogurt	**2 tbsp**
2 tbsp	olive oil	**2 tbsp**
250 g	mushrooms, wiped clean and quartered	**8 oz**
40 g	shallots, thinly sliced	**1½ oz**

1 tbsp	chopped fresh rosemary, or ¾ tsp dried rosemary	**1 tbsp**
¼ litre	red wine	**8 fl oz**
1	garlic clove, finely chopped	**1**
½ litre	unsalted brown or chicken stock	**16 fl oz**
¼ tsp	salt	**¼ tsp**
4 tbsp	double cream, mixed with 1 tbsp cornflour	**4 tbsp**

Preheat the oven to 240°C (475°F or Mark 9).

Spread the cracked peppercorns on a plate. Mix 2 tablespoons of the mustard with the yogurt and smear this mixture over the beef. Roll the beef in the peppercorns, coating it evenly on all sides. Place the beef on a rack set in a roasting pan. For medium-rare meat, cook the roast until a meat thermometer inserted in the centre registers 60°C (140°F)—about 35 minutes. Let the roast stand while you prepare the mushroom sauce.

Heat the oil in a large, heavy frying pan over medium heat. Add the mushrooms, shallots and rosemary, and cook them, stirring often, for 5 minutes. Add the wine and garlic, then rapidly boil the liquid until it is reduced by half—about 3 minutes. Stir in the stock and salt; reduce the sauce once again until only about 30 cl (½ pint) of liquid remains. Whisk in the cream-and cornflour mixture along with the remaining ½ tablespoon of mustard; simmer the sauce for 1 minute more to thicken it.

To serve, carve the roast into 20 very thin slices. Arrange the slices on a serving platter and pour the mushroom sauce over them.

Roast Fillet of Beef with Spinach and Sprouts

Serves 8

Working time: about 30 minutes

Total time: about 2 hours (includes marinating)

Calories
240
Protein
27g
Cholesterol
75mg
Total fat
12g
Saturated fat
4g
Sodium
160mg

1.25 kg	beef fillet in one piece, trimmed of fat	**2½ lb**
2 tbsp	toasted sesame seeds	**2 tbsp**
4 tbsp	low-sodium soy sauce or shoyu	**4 tbsp**
3 tbsp	rice vinegar or white wine vinegar	**3 tbsp**
1 tbsp	dark brown sugar	**1 tbsp**

1 tbsp	safflower oil	**1 tbsp**
350 g	fresh spinach, washed, stemmed and sliced into 5 mm (¼ inch) wide strips	**12 oz**
2	large ripe tomatoes, skinned, seeded and sliced into 5 mm (¼ inch) wide strips	**2**
400 g	bean sprouts	**14 oz**

Purée 1 tbsp sesame seeds, 3 tsps soy sauce, 2 tbsps vinegar, and the brown sugar in a blender. Put the fillet into a shallow dish, then pour on the marinade and leave for 1 hour, turning the meat occasionally.

Preheat the oven to 170°C (325°F or Mark 3). Drain the fillet, discarding the marinade, and pat it dry. Pour the oil into a large, shallow fireproof casserole set over high heat. Sear the meat until well browned on all sides—3 to 5 minutes. Place the casserole in the oven. For medium-rare meat, roast the beef for 40 to 45 minutes or until a meat thermometer inserted in the centre registers 60°C (140°F). Remove the meat from the oven and let it rest.

Heat a large frying pan or wok over medium heat. Add the spinach strips and cook them, stirring constantly, until their liquid has evaporated—2 to 3 minutes. Stir in the tomato strips and bean sprouts, and cook until heated through—3 to 4 minutes more. Remove the pan from the heat and stir in the remaining soy sauce and vinegar.

Cut the beef into 16 slices and arrange them on a platter with the spinach and bean sprout garnish. Sprinkle on the remaining sesame seeds and serve.

Roast Beef with Cloves and Red Peppers

Serves 12

Working time:
about 30
minutes

Total time:
about 2 hours

Calories
180
Protein
23g
Cholesterol
65mg
Total fat
7g
Saturated fat
2g
Sodium
155mg

1.75 kg	rolled beef topside	**3½ lb**
	or top rump, trimmed of fat	
4	sweet red peppers	**4**
1 tsp	ground cloves	**1 tsp**
1 tbsp	safflower oil	**1 tbsp**
½ tsp	salt	**½ tsp**

	freshly ground black pepper	
¼ litre	unsalted brown	**8 fl oz**
	or chicken stock	
500 g	white onions	**1 lb**
12.5 cl	dry white wine	**4 fl oz**

Grill the peppers until they are blackened on all sides—about 15 minutes. Transfer them to a bowl and cover it with plastic film to loosen their skins. Set aside.

Preheat the oven to 140°C (275°F or Mark 1) Sprinkle the meat with ½ tsp of the cloves.

Heat the oil in a large frying pan over high heat, then sear the beef until it is well browned on all sides—about 5 minutes. Transfer to a shallow fireproof casserole and sprinkle with ¼ tsp of salt and plenty of pepper. Roast the beef for 1 hour, adding small amounts of stock as necessary to prevent burning.

While the joint is roasting, peel the peppers, working over a bowl to catch the juice. Strain the juice and set aside. Slice the peppers into strips about 2.5 cm (1 inch) long and 1 cm (½ inch) wide. Half the onions from top to bottom, then slice them with the grain into strips like the pepper strips.

When the joint has cooked for 1 hour, add the peppers and their juice, the onions, stock, wine, remaining ground cloves and remaining salt. Roast the beef for 30 minutes more, or until a meat thermometer inserted into the centre registers 60°C (140°F).

Remove the roast from the oven and transfer the vegetables to a bowl. Boil the liquid remaining in the casserole until it is reduced to about 12.5 cl (4 fl oz). Slice and arrange them on a platter with the vegetables. Dribble the sauce over the beef and serve.

Peppered Veal Fillet

Serves 4	
Working time: about 20 minutes	
Total time: about 3 hours and 15 minutes (includes marinating)	

Calories 180	
Protein 40g	
Cholesterol 90mg	
Total fat 10g	
Saturated fat 2g	
Sodium 185mg	

500 g	veal fillet, trimmed of fat	**1 lb**
30 g	pumpkin seeds	**1 oz**
1 tsp	dried green peppercorns	**1 tsp**
½ tsp	black peppercorns	**½ tsp**
¼ tsp	hot red pepper flakes	**½ tsp**
1 tsp	Dijon mustard	**1 tsp**
350 g	ripe tomatoes, skinned, seeded and chopped, or 200 g (7 oz) canned tomatoes, drained and chopped watercress sprigs for garnish	**12 oz**

Toast the pumpkin seeds in a small, non-stick frying pan over medium heat, until golden-brown but not over-brown—stirring them with a long-handled spoon and standing well back because the seeds will snap and jump. Grind the toasted seeds finely in a blender or food processor.

Crush the green and black peppercorns and the pepper flakes finely in a mortar and pestle, then tip into a medium-sized bowl. Add the pumpkin seeds and the mustard, mix well, then add the tomatoes and bind to a wet paste. Place the veal fillet in the bowl and smear the paste all over it. Cover and marinate in the refrigerator for at least 2 hours.

Preheat the oven to 240°C (475°F or Mark 9).

Transfer the fillet to a small roasting pan and press on any pepper paste left in the bowl, checking that the ends are also covered. Roast for 10 minutes, then reduce the heat to 180°C (350°F or Mark 4) and continue roasting for 35 minutes longer. The veal should still be pink at this point; if you prefer the meat well done, roast for a further 10 to 15 minutes.

Remove the veal from the oven, cover loosely with foil and leave to rest in a warm place for 10 minutes. To serve, carve the veal into thick slices and garnish with watercress sprigs.

Stir-Fried Beef with Pine-Nuts on Chinese Cabbage

Serves 4

Working (and total time about 20 minutes)

Calories
225
Protein
19g
Cholesterol
55mg
Total fat
13g
Saturated fat
3g
Sodium
165mg

500 g	beef fillet, trimmed of fat and cut into thin strips	**1 lb**
4 tsp	cornflour	**4 tsp**
1 tsp	freshly ground black pepper	**1 tsp**
1 tsp	oyster sauce	**1 tsp**
1 tsp	low-sodium soy sauce or shoyu	**1 tsp**
1 tbsp	dry sherry	**1 tbsp**
½ tsp	sugar	**½ tsp**
1½ tbsp	safflower oil	**1½ tbsp**

60 g	onion, finely chopped	**2 oz**
½	sweet green pepper, seeded, deribbed and finely chopped	**½**
1	stick celery, finely chopped	**1**
1	spring onion, trimmed and thinly sliced	**1**
8	Chinese cabbage leaves, or iceberg lettuce leaves, washed and dried	**8**
2 tbsp	pine-nuts	**2 tbsp**

Put the beef strips into a bowl, and sprinkle them with 2 tsps cornflour and the pepper. Coat the strips and let them stand at room temperature while you prepare the remaining ingredients. In a small bowl, combine the remaining cornflour, the oyster sauce, soy sauce, sherry and sugar. Set aside.

Heat the oil in a large frying pan or wok. When the oil is hot, add the beef strips and stir-fry until the meat lightens but is still slightly pink—1 to 2 minutes. Use a slotted spoon to transfer the meat to a plate; set aside.

Return the pan to high heat. Add the onion, green pepper and celery and stir-fry for 30 seconds. Return the meat to the pan, then cook the mixture, stirring, until it is hot—10 to 15 secs. Pour the oyster-sauce mixture over the ingredients in the pan. Stir-fry the meat and vegetables until the sauce thickens and coats them—30 secs to 1 min. Remove from the heat.

Toss the spring onion with the beef and vegetables. Set two cabbage or lettuce leaves on each plate and divide the mixture among them. Sprinkle on the pine-nuts before serving.

Veal Chops with Spinach and Ricotta

Serves 4

Working time: about 45 minutes

Total time about 1 hour and 15 minutes

Calories 310
Protein 33g
Cholesterol 120mg
Total fat 17g
Saturated fat 5g
Sodium 290mg

4	veal loin chops (about 250 g/8 oz each), trimmed of fat	4
750 g	ripe tomatoes, skinned, seeded and chopped, or 400 g (14 oz) canned tomatoes, chopped	1½ lb
2	large fresh rosemary sprigs, or 1 tsp dried rosemary, crumbled	2
2 tbsp	virgin olive oil	2 tbsp
1	onion, finely chopped	1
125 g	fresh spinach leaves, chopped	4 oz
125 g	low-fat ricotta cheese	4 oz
⅛ tsp	grated nutmeg	⅛ tsp
¼ tsp	salt	¼ tsp
	freshly ground black pepper	
1	garlic clove, crushed	1
	rosemary sprigs for garnish (optional)	

Cut a pocket in the meaty part of each chop, through to the bone. Set aside. Put the tomatoes in a heavy-bottomed saucepan with the rosemary, adding a little water if using fresh tomatoes. Simmer for 10 minutes.

Meanwhile, heat 1 tbsp oil in a large frying pan. Add the onion and cook gently until softened—about 5 minutes. Add the spinach and stir, until it has wilted and the excess moisture has evaporated—3 to 4 minutes.

Transfer the spinach to a bowl. Add half the ricotta, the nutmeg, salt and some pepper, mix and set aside

Preheat the oven to 180°C (350°F or Mark

4). Mix together the remaining ricotta and the garlic; divide into four and stuff the pockets in the chops. Close the openings with wooden toothpicks

Heat the remaining oil in a large frying pan over medium-high heat and brown the chops on both sides—about 5 minutes in all. Transfer the chops to a baking dish. Spread the spinach and ricotta mixture over them. Discard the rosemary sprigs, and spoon the tomatoes over the chops and cheese mixture. Bake for 30 minutes. Remove the toothpicks and serve hot, garnished, if you like, with small rosemary sprigs.

Beef Barbecue Sandwiches

Serves 8

Working time:
about 45
minutes

Total time:
about 2 hours
and 30
minutes

Calories
380
Protein
34g
Cholesterol
85mg
Total fat
10g
Saturated fat
3g
Sodium
435mg

125 g	rolled beef topside or top rump, trimmed of fat	4 fl oz
800 g	canned whole tomatoes, puréed and sieved	1¼ lb
1	onion, finely chopped	1
17.5 cl	cider vinegar	6 fl oz
30 g	celery leaves, finely chopped	1 oz
1	lemon, juice only	1
4 tbsp	light brown sugar	4 tbsp
10	drops Tabasco sauce	10
¼ tsp	salt	¼ tsp

	freshly ground black pepper	
8	large soft bread rolls	8
	Coleslaw	
300 g	white cabbage, shredded	10 oz
1	small carrot, grated	1
1	red apple, grated	1
¼ litre	plain low-fat yogurt	8 fl oz
½ tsp	dry mustard	½ tsp
1 tsp	prepared horseradish	1 tsp
¼ tsp	salt	¼ tsp
½ tsp	celery seeds	½ tsp

Pour the puréed tomatoes into a large saucepan along with ¾ litre (1 ¼ pints) of water. Add the onion, vinegar and beef, and bring the liquid to a simmer over medium heat. Reduce the heat, cover the pan, leaving the lid slightly ajar, and simmer the mixture, stirring occasionally, for 1½ hours. If the tomato sauce begins to scorch, stir about 12.5 cl (4 fl oz) of water into it.

To make the coleslaw, toss the cabbage in a bowl with the carrot, apple, yogurt, mustard,

horseradish, salt and celery seeds. Cover the bowl and refrigerate it.

When the meat is done, remove it from the saucepan and let it sit at room temperature. Add the celery leaves, lemon juice, brown sugar, Tabasco sauce, salt and some pepper to the tomato mixture. Coarsely chop the beef and add it also. Simmer the barbecue beef over low heat for 30 minutes.

Split the rolls and fill them with the beef, topped with some of the coleslaw.

Beef and Wheat Berry Salad

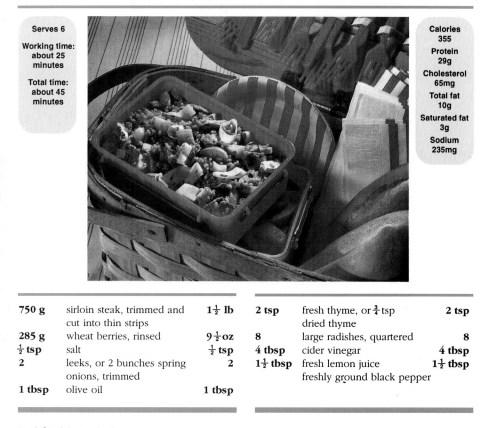

750 g	sirloin steak, trimmed and cut into thin strips	**1½ lb**
285 g	wheat berries, rinsed	**9½ oz**
½ tsp	salt	**½ tsp**
2	leeks, or 2 bunches spring onions, trimmed	**2**
1 tbsp	olive oil	**1 tbsp**
2 tsp	fresh thyme, or ¾ tsp dried thyme	**2 tsp**
8	large radishes, quartered	**8**
4 tbsp	cider vinegar	**4 tbsp**
1½ tbsp	fresh lemon juice freshly ground black pepper	**1½ tbsp**

Boil 60 cl (1 pint) of water in a saucepan. Add the wheat berries and ¼ tsp of the salt. Reduce the heat and cover the pan, leaving the lid ajar. Simmer the wheat berries until tender—about 45 minutes. Drain them and set them aside.

Meanwhile, if using leeks, slice them into rounds about 1 cm (½ inch) wide. Wash the rounds in two or three changes of cold water. Drain the rounds and set them aside. (If using spring onions, simply slice them.)

Ten minutes before the wheat berries are ready, heat 2 tsps of the oil in a large frying pan over high heat. Add the beef and thyme, and cook, stirring frequently, for 2 minutes; then transfer to a large bowl.

Return the pan to the heat and add the remaining teaspoon of oil. Add the leeks or spring onions and the radishes, and cook them, stirring frequently, for 3 minutes. Pour in the vinegar, lemon juice, the reserved beef and wheat berries, the remaining salt, and a generous grinding of black pepper. Continue cooking, stirring frequently, for 1 minute more. With a slotted spoon, transfer the mixture to a large serving bowl.

Return the pan to high heat and boil the liquid until it is reduced to 4 tablespoons. Pour the reduced liquid over the salad and toss well. Serve the salad warm or chilled.

Beef Fillet Stir-Fried with Butternut Squash and Turnips

Serves 4

Working time:
about 15
minutes

Total time:
about 25
minutes

Calories
215
Protein
20g
Cholesterol
55mg
Total fat
10g
Saturated fat
3g
Sodium
235mg

500 g	beef fillet trimmed and sliced into 5 cm (2 inch) long strips	**1 lb**	**2 tbsp**	chopped fresh tarragon, or 2 tsp dried tarragon	**2 tbsp**
30 cl	unsalted brown or chicken stock	**½ pint**	**1**	small onion, thinly sliced	**1**
250 g	turnips, peeled, quartered and cut into 5 mm (¼ inch) thick slices freshly ground black pepper	**8 oz**	**¼ tsp**	salt	**¼ tsp**
			1 tbsp	safflower oil	**1 tbsp**
350 g	butternut squash, peeled, cut into 5 mm (¼ inch) slices	**12 oz**	**1**	garlic clove, finely chopped	**1**
			1 tsp	cornflour, mixed with 1 tbsp water	**1 tsp**
			1 tsp	distilled white vinegar	**1 tsp**

Put the stock and onion in a saucepan. Set a vegetable steamer in the pan and bring the stock to a simmer. Sprinkle the turnips and squash with 1 tblsp of the fresh tarragon or all of the dried. Put the turnips in the steamer for 2 minutes. Add the squash and continue steaming until tender—about 3 minutes. Transfer the vegetables to a plate and set aside, and reserve the stock and onion.

Season the beef with the salt and pepper. Heat ½ tbsp of the oil in a wok or a frying pan over high heat, and sear the beef, tossing to prevent it from sticking, for about 2 minutes. Turn off the heat, transfer the meat to a plate, and keep it warm. Wipe out the wok or pan and set it over high heat again. Add the remaining oil, the garlic and vegetables, and cook them, stirring continuously, for 3 minutes. Add the beef, toss well, and push the ingredients to the sides of the pan. Pour in the stock and onions, and bring to a simmer. Whisk in the cornflour mixture and the vinegar, whisking continuously until the liquid thickens—about 2 minutes. Serve the beef and vegetables with the sauce. If using fresh tarragon, sprinkle the remainder over the top.

Entrecôte Steak with Mushrooms and Red Onions

Serves 8

Working time:
about 1 hour

Total time:
about 3 hours
(includes
marinating)

Calories
245
Protein
29g
Cholesterol
70mg
Total fat
8g
Saturated fat
3g
Sodium
70mg

1.25 kg	entrecôte or rumpsteak in one piece, trimmed of fat	**2½ lb**	**20**	juniper berries		**20**
2	red onions, thickly sliced	**2**	**500 g**	fresh mushrooms,		**1 lb**
35 cl	red wine	**12 fl oz**	**17.5 cl**	unsalted brown or chicken stock		**6 fl oz**
4 tbsp	raspberry vinegar or distilled white vinegar	**4 tbsp**	**2 tbsp**	cornflour		**2 tbsp**
				freshly ground black pepper		
4 tbsp	fresh lime juice	**4 tbsp**	**4 tbsp**	finely chopped parsley		**4 tbsp**

Spread the onion slices in the bottom of a shallow baking dish. Set the steak on the onions. Pour the wine, vinegar and lime juice on the steak, then scatter the juniper berries over all. Let the steak marinate at room temperature for 2 hours.

Remove the steak and onions from the marinade, and pat dry. Strain the marinade into a bowl and set aside. Discard the berries.

Heat a large, frying pan over high heat. Add the onion slices and sauté until they are tender—about 4 minutes each side. Remove them from the pan and keep them warm. Cook the steak over medium-high heat for 4 minutes on each side for medium-rare meat.

Remove the steak from the pan and let it rest while you prepare the mushrooms.

Sauté the mushrooms until most of the juices have evaporated—about 5 minutes. Remove them with a slotted spoon and set them aside. Pour the marinade into the pan and boil it until it has reduced by half—about 10 minutes. Mix the stock and the cornflour and whisk into the reduced marinade. Bring the liquid to the boil and continue cooking until it thickens—about 1 minute. Season the mushrooms with some black pepper and stir them, along with the parsley, into the sauce

Slice the steak and serve with the mushrooms spooned round it.

Beef Stroganoff with Wild Mushrooms

Serves 4

Working time:
about 40
minutes

Total time:
about 1 hour

Calories
220
Protein
24g
Cholesterol
50mg
Total fat
12g
Saturated fat
3g
Sodium
150mg

350 g	beef fillet, trimmed of fat	**12 oz**
15 g	dried ceps (porcini), or other wild mushrooms, soaked in 15 cl ($\frac{3}{4}$ pint) warm water for 20 minutes	**$\frac{1}{2}$ oz**
2 tbsp	virgin olive oil	**2 tbsp**
125 g	shallots, thinly sliced	**4 oz**
$\frac{1}{4}$ tsp	salt	**$\frac{1}{4}$ tsp**
125 g	button mushrooms, sliced	

$\frac{1}{2}$ tsp	dried green peppercorns, crushed	**$\frac{1}{2}$ tsp**
5 tbsp	Greek-style strained yogurt	**5 tbsp**
$\frac{1}{2}$ tsp	Dijon mustard	**$\frac{1}{2}$ tsp**
2	firm ripe tomatoes, skinned, seeded and cut into thin strips	**2**
1	small gherkin, cut into short thin strips	**1**

Cut the beef fillets crosswise (against the grain) into slices about 5 mm ($\frac{1}{4}$ inch) thick. Cut the slices into strips about 4 cm ($\frac{1}{2}$ inch) long. Drain the soaked mushrooms, reserving the soaking water, and remove any remaining sand or grit under running water; then chop coarsely. Strain the soaking water through a sieve lined with paper towels.

Heat 2 teaspoons of the oil in a large, non-stick frying pan over medium heat. Add the shallots and cook for 2 minutes, stirring, then add the wild mushrooms, soaking water and button mushrooms Cook, stirring frequently, until the excess liquid has evaporated—

about 10 minutes. Remove the mushroom mixture from the pan. Heat another 2 teaspoons of the oil in the pan over high heat and add half the beef. Fry briskly for 3 to 4 minutes, stirring and tossing to brown the strips evenly. Add the browned strips to the mushroom mixture. Heat the remaining oil in the pan and brown the remaining beef strips in the same way. Return the first batch of beef and the mushroom mixture to the pan and stir. Mix in the peppercorns and salt.

Mix together the yogurt and mustard. Add to the pan with the tomato and gherkin strips. Fold together gently and heat through.

Sautéed Beef Tossed with Red Cabbage and Apples

Serves 8

Working time: about 30 minutes

Total time: about 45 minutes

Calories 220

Protein 19g

Cholesterol 50mg

Total fat 7g

Saturated fat 2g

Sodium 145mg

850 g	sirloin steak, trimmed and cut into thin strips about 4 cm (1½ inches) long	1¾ lb
45 g	shallots, chopped	1½ oz
1.25 kg	red cabbage, cored, quartered and sliced	2½ lb
2	tart green apples, cored, and cut into strips 5 cm (2 inches) long and 5 mm (¼ inch) wide	2
¼ tsp	salt	¼ tsp
½ litre	red wine	16 fl oz
2 tsp	caraway seeds	2 tsp
1 tbsp	honey	1 tbsp
¼ litre	unsalted brown or chicken stock	8 fl oz
4 tbsp	fresh lemon juice	4 tbsp
1 tsp	freshly ground black pepper	1 tsp
1½ tbsp	safflower oil	1½ tbsp
2	spring onions, sliced	2

Combine the shallots, salt, stock, wine and 1 tsp of the caraway seeds in a non-reactive saucepan over medium heat. Simmer the liquid until it is reduced to 12.5 cl (4 fl oz)—about 40 minutes. Meanwhile, place the cabbage in a bowl with the apples and the remaining caraway seeds. Mix the honey and lemon juice, and pour it over the cabbage mixture. Toss the mixture well and set.aside.

Place the meat in a bowl and sprinkle it with the pepper. Pour the reduced liquid over the meat and stir the mixture well.

Heat 1 tablespoon of the oil in a large sauté pan or heavy frying pan set over high heat. Add the beef and spring onions and sauté them, stirring, until the meat is browned—about 1½ minutes. Transfer the mixture to a bowl.

Heat the remaining oil in the pan over medium-high heat. Add the cabbage-and-apple mixture and cook it, stirring frequently, until the cabbage has wilted slightly—3 to 4 minutes. Return the beef to the pan, toss the mixture well, and serve it at once.

Medallions of Veal with Rosemary and Red Wine

Serves 6

Working time: about 15 minutes

Total time: about 1 hour and 15 minutes (includes marinating)

Calories 200

Protein 21g

Cholesterol 95mg

Total fat 12g

Saturated fat 3g

Sodium 215mg

6	medallions of veal, trimmed (about 125 g/4 oz each)	**6**
	fresh rosemary sprigs	
2 tbsp	virgin olive oil	**2 tbsp**
1	garlic clove, crushed	**1**
1	lemon, finely grated rind only	**1**
1 tbsp	chopped parsley	**1 tbsp**
15 g	unsalted butter	**½ oz**
¼ litre	red wine	**8 fl oz**
15 cl	unsalted veal or chicken stock	**¼ pint**
¼ tsp	salt	**¼ tsp**
	freshly ground black pepper	

Spear each medallion of veal with two or three small sprigs of rosemary. Blend 1½ tablespoons of the oil with the garlic, lemon rind and parsley in a shallow dish. Add the medallions to this marinade and turn them carefully until they are well coated. Cover and marinate at room temperature for at least 1 hour.

Heat the remaining oil with the butter in a non-stick sauté or frying pan. Add the medallions and cook for 2 to 3 minutes on each side until well browned but still slightly pink inside. Transfer the veal to a plate lined with absorbent paper towels. Cover and keep hot.

Pour off all the excess fat from the sauté pan, and stir in the wine and stock. Bring to the boil, stirring, then boil gently until the liquid is reduced by half. Season with the salt and some pepper.

Arrange the medallions on a hot serving plate, strain the sauce over them and, if liked, garnish with more rosemary sprigs. Serve immediately.

Veal Fillets with Gorgonzola and Fennel

Serves 4

Working
(and total)
time: about
40 minutes

Calories
240
Protein
27g
Cholesterol
105mg
Total fat
12g
Saturated fat
2g
Sodium
380mg

500 g	veal fillet, trimmed, cut diagonally into 5 mm ($\frac{1}{4}$ inch) slices and slightly flattened	**1 lb**
1 tbsp	virgin olive oil	**1 tbsp**
2 tbsp	Pernod or unsalted stock	**2 tbsp**
250 g	bulb fennel, cut into slices, feathery tops reserved	**8 oz**

90 g	Gorgonzola cheese, mashed	**3 oz**
2 tbsp	skimmed milk	**2 tbsp**
2 tsp	fresh sage, or $\frac{1}{2}$ tsp dried sage	**2 tsp**
2 tsp	chopped fresh thyme, or $\frac{1}{2}$ tsp dried thyme	**2 tsp**
$\frac{1}{8}$ tsp	salt	**$\frac{1}{8}$ tsp**
	freshly ground black pepper	

Preheat the oven to 140°C (275°F or Mark 1). Heat the oil in a non-stick frying pan over medium-high heat, add as many pieces of veal as the pan will comfortably hold and cook for 3 to 5 minutes until just tender, turning once and pressing the pieces of veal firmly with a palette knife or spatula to keep them as flat as possible. Transfer the veal to a platter, cover and keep hot in the oven. Cook the remainder of the veal in the same way.

Add the Pernod or stock to the cooking juices in the pan, increase the heat and stir briskly to deglaze. Add the fennel and toss over high heat for 2 to 3 minutes, then remove with a slotted spoon and keep hot with the veal.

Reduce the heat, add the Gorgonzola and milk, and cook gently, stirring, until the cheese has melted and formed a sauce with the cooking juices and milk. Add the chopped sage, thyme, salt and some pepper, and remove the pan from the heat.

To assemble the dish, arrange the meat and fennel on individual plates. Spoon the sauce over the meat and garnish with the reserved fennel tops. Serve immediately.

Sauerbraten

Serves 6

Working time about 45 minutes

Total time: about 3 days (includes marinating)

Calories
340
Protein
40g
Cholesterol
75mg
Total fat
6g
Saturated fat
3g
Sodium
200mg

1 kg	beef topside, rolled and tied	2 lb
10	whole cloves	10
¼ litre	red wine	8 fl oz
12.5 cl	red wine vinegar	4 fl oz
1	onion, grated	1
2 tsp	soft brown sugar	2 tsp
1 tsp	dry mustard	1 tsp
6	black peppercorns	6
2	bay leaves	2

½ tsp	ground allspice	½ tsp
1 tbsp	virgin olive oil	1 tbsp
30 cl	brown stock	½ pint
1.5 kg	mixed root vegetables	3 lb
3 tbsp	raisins	3 tbsp
2 tsp	arrowroot	2 tsp
	freshly ground black pepper	
⅛ tsp	salt	⅛ tsp
2 tbsp	finely chopped parsley	2 tbsp

Stud the beef with cloves and place in an earthenware dish. In a saucepan, heat the wine, wine vinegar, onion, sugar, mustard, peppercorns, bay leaves and allspice. Pour over the beef and leave to marinate in the refrigerator for 3 days, turning occasionally.

30 minutes before cooking, remove the beef, pat it dry and leave at room temperature. Reserve the marinade. Preheat the oven to 150°C (300°F or Mark 2).

Heat the oil in a fireproof casserole and brown the beef. Strain the marinade over the beef, add the stock and bring to the boil. Cover

and cook in the oven for 1¼ hours, turning and basting often. Meanwhile, put the vegetables in a large saucepan of water, bring to the boil and set aside. Remove the casserole from the oven and arrange the vegetables round the meat. Cover and return to the oven for 1 hour.

After which transfer the dish to the stovetop and add raisins. Mix the arrowroot with 1 tablespoon of cold water and stir into the cooking liquid. Bring to the boil, stirring, then simmer until thickened and season. Serve the meat sliced, with a little gravy. Serve the vegetables and remaining gravy separately.

Beef Braised in Beer

1.25 kg	beef topside, trimmed of fat	**2½ lb**	**4**	garlic cloves, chopped	**4**
½ tsp	safflower oil	**½ tsp**	**2 tbsp**	julienned fresh ginger root	**2 tbsp**
2 kg	large onions, sliced	**4 lb**	**1**	bay leaf	**1**
½ litre	unsalted brown or chicken stock	**16 fl oz**	**4**	fresh thyme sprigs, or 1 tsp dried thyme	**4**
2 tbsp	plain flour	**2 tbsp**	**1**	strip lemon rind	**1**
35 cl	stout	**12 fl oz**	**2 tbsp**	dark molasses	**2 tbsp**
			½ tsp	salt	**½ tsp**
				freshly ground black pepper	

Preheat the oven to 170°C (325°F or Mark 3). Heat the oil in a large frying pan over high heat. Add the joint and sear until well browned—about 5 minutes in all. Transfer to an ovenproof casserole

Reduce the heat under the pan to medium. Add the onions and cook them until they begin to soften—about 10 minutes. Deglaze the pan with 2 tbsps of the stock. Continue cooking the onions, adding another 2 tbsps of stock when necessary, until they are very soft and their juices have caramelized—15 to 20 minutes more. Sprinkle the flour over the onions, stirring constantly, for 1 minute.

Pour ¼ litre (8 fl oz) of the remaining stock into the pan and stir well. Increase the heat to medium high and boil until quite thick—3 to 4 minutes. Pour in the rest of the stock and the stout. Bring to a simmer, then transfer the contents of the pan to the casserole. Add the garlic, ginger, bay leaf, thyme, lemon rind, molasses, salt and some pepper. Cover and braise the joint in the oven until it is very tender—about 2 hours.

Slice and arrange the beef on a serving platter. Remove the bay leaf, the thyme sprigs and the lemon rind from the sauce, and pour it over the meat.

Roulades in Tomato Sauce

Serves 8

Working time:
about 1 hour
30 minutes

Total time:
about 4 hours

Calories
235
Protein
25g
Cholesterol
55mg
Total fat
8g
Saturated fat
3g
Sodium
165mg

1 kg	beef topside, trimmed and cut diagonally into 16 slices	2 lb
1 tsp	safflower oil	1 tsp
3	onions, finely chopped	3
4	garlic cloves, finely chopped	4
2	carrots, finely chopped	2
1.5 kg	canned whole tomatoes, with their juice	3 lb
2	bay leaves	2
3 tbsp	chopped parsley	3 tbsp
2 tbsp	chopped fresh oregano, or 2 tsp dried oregano	2 tbsp
45 g	dry breadcrumbs	1½ oz
4 tbsp	freshly grated Parmesan cheese	4 tbsp
2 tbsp	finely chopped prosciutto or cooked ham	2 tbsp
4 tbsp	dry white wine	4 tbsp

Mix the oil, onions, garlic and carrots in a large, heavy-bottomed saucepan. Cover, and cook the mixture over low heat until the onions are translucent—about 15 minutes.

Purée the tomatoes in a food processor or a blender. Add the purée and bay leaves to the onion-and-carrot mixture. Increase the heat to medium and simmer the vegetables, uncovered, until they become a thick sauce—about 2 hours.

While the sauce is simmering, make the roulades. In a bowl, combine the parsley, oregano, breadcrumbs, cheese, prosciutto or ham, and the wine. Spread the beef slices flat on the work surface and spread some of the stuffing mixture on each one. Roll up each slice and tie it with two short pieces of string to secure it.

Add the roulades to the thickened sauce and simmer them until the meat is tender—about 1 hour. Lift the roulades from the sauce and remove the string. Spoon the sauce over the roulades and serve them immediately.

Cabbage Rolls with Beef and Sage

Serves 6

Working time:
about 30
minutes

Total time:
about 2 hours

Calories
305

Protein
27g

Cholesterol
60mg

Total fat
9g

Saturated fat
3g

Sodium
250mg

750 g	beef topside, trimmed, cut diagonally into 12 thin slices	**1½ lb**
1	large green cabbage	**1**
1 tbsp	safflower oil	**1 tbsp**
350 g	onion, chopped	**12 oz**
1 tbsp	chopped fresh sage, or 1 tsp dried sage	**1 tbsp**
4	garlic cloves, finely chopped	**4**
3	slices white bread, crumbled	**3**
30 g	stemmed parsley sprigs	**1 oz**
800 g	canned whole tomatoes,	**1¾ lb**
3	carrots, thinly sliced	**3**
3 tbsp	cider vinegar	**3 tbsp**
1½ tbsp	sugar	**1½ tbsp**
¼ tsp	salt	**¼ tsp**
	freshly ground black pepper	

Boil twelve outer leaves of the cabbage, with cores removed, until they are limp—about 10 minutes, then drain. Finely slice 450 g (15 oz) of the remaining cabbage.

Heat the safflower oil in a large frying pan over medium heat. Add the sliced cabbage, 275 g (9 oz) of the onion, 2 tsps of fresh sage or ½ tsp dried sage, and half of the garlic. Cook, stirring occasionally, until the cabbage is soft—about 10 minutes. Put the mixture in a bowl with the crumbled bread and the parsley, and toss well. Set the filling aside.

Meanwhile, put the tomatoes and their juice, the remaining garlic, the carrots and 17.5 cl (6 fl oz) of water into a large frying

pan. Gently cook for 15 minutes. Add the remaining onion, the vinegar, the sugar, the remaining sage, the salt and some pepper. Let this simmer while you prepare the rolls.

Shape the beef slices to a thickness of 3 mm (⅛ inch) and sprinkle with black pepper.

Set a cabbage leaf on a work surface with the stem end towards you. Lay a beef slice on top of the leaf, then mound 2 heaped tablespoons of the filling on the beef. Roll up, starting at the stem end; folding in the sides.

Place the rolls, seam sides down, in the sauce and cook, with the pan lid slightly ajar for 1¼ hours. Carefully transfer the rolls to a platter. Spoon the sauce over them and serve.

Braised Cinnamon Beef Roll

Serves 4

Working time: about 25 minutes

Total time: about 2 hours

Calories
250
Protein
28g
Cholesterol
70mg
Total fat
11g
Saturated fat
3g
Sodium
215mg

600 g	beef topside, trimmed and cut into four slices	**1¼ tsp**
1 tbsp	ground cinnamon	**1 tbsp**
¼ tsp	salt	**¼ tsp**
	freshly ground black pepper	
1 tbsp	safflower oil	**1 tbsp**
1	large onion, thinly sliced	**1**
1	garlic clove, finely chopped	**1**
2	cinnamon sticks	**2**
12.5 cl	dry white wine	**4 fl oz**
¼ litre	unsalted brown or chicken stock	**8 fl oz**
1 tbsp	cornflower, mixed with 1 tbsp of the stock	**1 tbsp**

Using 2 polythene sheets, pound the beef to a thickness of 3 mm (⅛ inch). Sprinkle with ground cinnamon, salt and pepper. Overlap the edges of two slices, spiced side up; cover the seam thus formed with polythene or greaseproof paper and lightly pound the overlapping edges to join the slices. Repeat for the other slices.

Place one of the joined pieces on top of the other, spiced side up, then roll up tightly, starting with one of the longer edges. Use string to hold together.

Heat 1 teaspoon of the oil in a sauté pan over medium-high heat and sear the beef on all sides. Remove the meat; add the remaining 2 teaspoons of oil and the onion

to the pan and cook the onion over medium heat until it is translucent—4 to 5 minutes. Stir in the garlic, cinnamon sticks, wine and stock. Return the beef to the pan and, if needed, pour in enough water to half submerge the roll. Bring to a simmer, cover tightly, and leave until the meat feels tender—1¼ to 1½ hours.

When cooked, transfer to a plate. Increase the heat to medium high and bring the liquid to the boil. Discard the cinnamon sticks. Whisk in the cornflour paste, whisking continuously until the sauce thickens—about 30 seconds.

Remove the string, slice the meat thinly, and place the slices on a serving platter. Top them with some of the sauce, pouring the rest round the beef. Serve immediately.

Spicy Beef Stew with Apricots and Olives

Serves 8

Working time: about 30 minutes

Total time: about 2 hours and 30 minutes

Calories 290

Protein 29g

Cholesterol 70mg

Total fat 11g

Saturated fat 3g

Sodium 275mg

1.25 kg	beef topside, trimmed of fat and cut into cubes	2½ lb	12.5 cl	red wine	4 fl oz	
			4	garlic cloves, chopped	4	
1 tbsp	safflower oil	1 tbsp	1½ tsp	ground cumin	1½ tsp	
3	onions, chopped	3	1½ tsp	ground coriander	1½ tsp	
400 g	canned whole tomatoes, chopped, with their juice	14 oz	1⅛ tsp	cayenne pepper	1⅛ tsp	
			125 g	dried apricots, halved	4 oz	
½ litre	unsalted brown or chicken stock	16 fl oz	16	green olives, stoned, rinsed and drained	16	

Heat the oil in a large, heavy frying pan over medium heat. Add the onions and cook them, stirring often, until translucent—about 5 minutes. With a slotted spoon, transfer the onions to a fireproof casserole.

Increase the heat to medium high. Add the beef cubes to the frying pan and brown them on all sides—5 to 7 minutes.

Transfer the beef to the casserole and add the garlic, the tomatoes and their juice, the stock, wine, cumin, coriander and cayenne pepper. Cover the casserole and reduce the heat to low; simmer the beef, stirring occasionally, for 1½ hours.

Stir the apricots and olives into the casserole, and continue cooking the stew until the meat is tender—about 30 minutes more. Transfer the stew to a bowl or a deep platter, and serve.

Japanese Simmered Beef

Serves 6

Working time:
about 25
minutes

Total time:
about 40
minutes

Calories
230
Protein
20g
Cholesterol
35mg
Total fat
7g
Saturated fat
2g
Sodium
350mg

500 g	beef fillet, trimmed and sliced against the grain	**1 lb**
125 g	Japanese udon noodles or vermicelli	**4 oz**
1	large carrot, diagonally sliced	**1**
60 g	shiitake or other fresh mushrooms, the stems discarded and caps sliced	**2 oz**
3	spring onions, julienned	**3**
90 g	Chinese cabbage, cut · into chiffonade	**3 oz**

250 g	tofu, cut into 2 cm (¾ inch) wide strips	**8 oz**
1.5 litres	unsalted brown or chicken stock	**2½ pints**
2 tbsp	low-sodium soy sauce or shoyu	**2 tbsp**
2 tbsp	rice vinegar	**2 tbsp**
1 tsp	finely chopped fresh ginger root	**1 tsp**
1 tsp	finely chopped garlic	**1 tsp**
¼ tsp	dark sesame oil	**¼ tsp**

Cook the noodles (or vermicelli) in 2 litres (3½ pints) of boiling water until they are *al dente*. Drain them and rinse under running water to keep them from sticking. Drain again and set them aside in a bowl.

Arrange the beef slices, the vegetables and the tofu on a large plate.

Combine the stock, soy sauce, vinegar, ginger and garlic in an electric frying pan, a wok or fondue pot. Bring to a simmer and

cook for 5 minutes, then add the sesame oil.

Begin the meal by cooking pieces of the beef briefly in the simmering broth—30 seconds to 1 minute. After the meat has been eaten, cook the vegetables and tofu in the broth just until they are warmed through—3 to 4 minutes. Finish the meal with the noodles or vermicelli, adding them to the broth and heating them. They may be eaten with the broth or served on their own.

Blanquette of Veal

Serves 4

Working time:
about 50
minutes

Total time:
about 2 hours

Calories
190
Protein
20g
Cholesterol
125mg
Total fat
7g
Saturated fat
3g
Sodium
250mg

350 g	topside of veal or top rump, trimmed and cubed	**12 oz**
8	pearl onions or shallots	**8**
8	button mushrooms, wiped clean	**8**
1	stick celery, cut into chunks	**1**
1	fresh thyme sprig, or	**1**
	$\frac{1}{2}$ tsp dried thyme	**1**
1	bay leaf	**1**
2	parsley sprigs	**2**

60 cl	unsalted veal or chicken stock	**1 pint**
8	small carrots	**8**
1 tbsp	cornflour	**1 tbsp**
$\frac{1}{4}$ litre	semi-skimmed milk	**8 fl oz**
1	egg yolk	**1**
1 tbsp	lemon juice	**1 tbsp**
$\frac{1}{2}$ tsp	salt	**$\frac{1}{2}$ tsp**
	white pepper	

Put the veal into a heavy, medium-sized saucepan and cover with cold water. Bring to the boil, then drain. Return the veal to the pan and add the onions, mushrooms, celery, thyme, bay leaf, parsley sprigs and stock. Bring to the boil, reduce the heat, cover and simmer for 25 minutes. Add the carrots and simmer for a further 20 minutes. Remove the veal and vegetables with a slotted spoon and set aside. Discard the herbs and strain the stock into a clean pan. Boil to reduce to 30 cl ($\frac{1}{2}$ pint)—10 to 15 minutes.

Dissolve the cornflour in a little of the milk. Add the remaining milk to the stock and bring back to the boil. Reduce the heat, whisk in the cornflour mixture and simmer for 10 minutes, stirring. Lightly beat the egg yolk with the lemon juice in a small bowl. Stir in a little of the hot sauce and stir this into the remaining sauce in the pan. Cook gently, stirring, for 1 minute. Add the salt and some white pepper. Return the veal and vegetables to the sauce and heat through gently without boiling. Serve hot.

Spicy Minced Meat on a Bed of Sweet Potatoes

Serves 4

Working time: about 1 hour

Total time: about 2 hours and 30 minutes

Calories 522
Protein 35g
Cholesterol 75mg
Total fat 10g
Saturated fat 3g
Sodium 260mg

600 g	beef topside, trimmed and minced	**1¼ lb**
4	orange-fleshed sweet potatoes	**4**
1.5 kg	ripe tomatoes, chopped	**3 lb**
2	bay leaves	**2**
2	cinnamon sticks	**2**
4	allspice berries	**4**
8	black peppercorns	**8**
2	dried red chili peppers, or ¼ tsp cayenne pepper	**2**
1 tbsp	tomato paste	**1 tbsp**
1 tsp	safflower oil	**1 tsp**
1	onion, finely chopped	**1**
¼ tsp	salt	**¼ tsp**
2 tbsp	chopped parsley	**2 tbsp**
12.5 cl	plain low-fat yogurt	**4 fl oz**

Preheat the oven 200°C (400°F or Mark 6). Bake the sweet potatoes for 1 hour or until they are tender.

Meanwhile, put the tomatoes, bay leaves, cinnamon sticks, allspice berries, peppercorns, and chili peppers or cayenne pepper into a heavy pan. Bring to the boil, then simmer it until it is reduced to 1½ litre (16 fl oz)—about 1½ hours. Discard the cinnamon sticks and bay leaves from the tomato sauce, and put it through a sieve. Set aside.

Sauté the beef in a large, frying pan over high heat. When evenly browned—about 5 minutes—add the tomato sauce and paste.

Simmer until most of the liquid has evaporated—about 20 minutes. Pour the meat sauce into a bowl and keep warm.

Peel the baked sweet potatoes and chop them coarsely. Wipe out the frying pan, pour in the oil and heat gently. Add the onion and cook it until it is translucent—about 5 minutes. Add the sweet potatoes and 4 tbsps of water, and cook, stirring frequently, over medium heat until the water is absorbed—about 5 minutes; stir in the salt and chopped parsley.

Place the sweet potatoes on a serving platter and top them with the meat. Serve immediately, passing the yogurt separately.

Burghul-Stuffed Red Peppers

Serves 4

Working time:
about 25
minutes

Total time:
about 45
minutes

Calories
285
Protein
20g
Cholesterol
40mg
Total fat
9g
Saturated fat
2g
Sodium
210mg

350 g	beef topside, trimmed and minced	**12 oz**
4	large sweet red or green peppers	**4**
4 tsp	olive oil	**4 tsp**
1	onion, chopped	**1**
2 tsp	fresh thyme, or $\frac{1}{2}$ tsp dried	**2 tsp**
125 g	mushrooms, thinly sliced	
2 tbsp	finely chopped celery	**2 tbsp**

125 g	burghul	**4 fl oz**
$\frac{1}{4}$ tsp	salt	**$\frac{1}{4}$ tsp**
	freshly ground black pepper	
35 cl	unsalted brown or chicken stock	**12 fl oz**
1	garlic clove, finely chopped	**1**
2 tbsp	sherry vinegar or red wine vinegar	**2 tbsp**

Preheat the oven to 200°C (400°C or Mark 6).

Seed and derib the peppers Slice off the tops, dice them, and set the pieces aside.

Heat 1 tablespoon of the oil in a heavy saucepan over medium heat. Add half of the onion, half of the thyme, the mushrooms, celery, burghul, $\frac{1}{8}$ teaspoon of the salt and some pepper. Cook the vegetables and burghul, stirring frequently, for 5 minutes. Add the stock, stir the mixture well, and cover the pan. Cook the mixture, stirring it occasionally, until the liquid is absorbed—about 12 minutes.

In a non-stick frying pan. heat the remaining oil over medium-high heat. When the pan is hot, add the beef, the reserved diced peppers, the remaining onion, the remaining thyme and the garlic. Cook, stirring frequently, until the beef is browned—5 to 7 minutes. Add the remaining salt, some freshly ground pepper and the vinegar. Cook for 30 seconds, then remove it from the heat.

Combine the burghul mixture with the beef and fill the peppers, mounding the filling. Bake the stuffed peppers in a shallow casserole, loosely covered with aluminium foil, for 25 minutes. Allow the peppers to stand for 5 minutes before serving them.

Beef Stew with Apricots and Couscous

Serves 4

Working time:
about 10
minutes

Total time:
about 1 hour
and 15
minutes

Calories
475
Protein
34g
Cholesterol
75mg
Total fat
10g
Saturated fat
3g
Sodium
450mg

½ tsp	salt	½ tsp	
	freshly ground black pepper		
500 g	lean stewing beef, cut into 2.5 cm (1 inch) cubes	1 lb	
2 tbsp	plain flour	2 tbsp	
1 tbsp	safflower oil	1 tbsp	
1	small onion, thinly sliced	1	
1	garlic clove, finely chopped	1	

12.5 cl	dry vermouth	4 fl oz
½ tsp	ground cinnamon	½ tsp
175 g	dried apricots, cut in half if large	6 oz
¾ litre	unsalted brown stock	1¼ pints
500 g	peas, shelled, or 145 g (5 oz) frozen peas, thawed	1 lb
175 g	couscous	6 oz

Sprinkle ¼ tsp salt and some pepper over the beef, then dredge them in the flour.

Heat the oil in a large, fireproof casserole over medium-high heat. Add the beef cubes and sauté them, turning them frequently, until browned on all sides—about 3 minutes. Push the beef to one side of the pan; reduce the heat, add the onion and garlic, and cook, stirring often, until the onion is translucent—about 4 minutes. Stir in the vermouth and cinnamon. Scrape the bottom of the pan with a wooden spoon to dissolve the caramelized juices and bits of flour. Simmer the liquid until it thickens—2 to 3 minutes.

Stir in one third of the apricots and half of the stock. Gently simmer, covered, for 30 minutes. Stir in the remaining stock and cook, covered, for 20 minutes more. Add the remaining apricots and the fresh peas, if you are using them. Cook the stew for 10 minutes more; if using frozen peas, stir them in about 3 minutes before the end of the cooking time.

To prepare the couscous, bring 35 cl (12 fl oz) of water to the boil in a small saucepan with the remaining salt. Remove the pan from the heat, stir in the couscous and leave, covered, for 5 minutes. Fluff the couscous with a fork and serve it with the stew.

Braised Veal

Serves 8

Working time: about 40 minutes

Total time: about 2 hours and 40 minutes

Calories 305
Protein 33g
Cholesterol 90mg
Total fat 8g
Saturated fat 3g
Sodium 210mg

1 kg	veal topside, trimmed and tied	**2 to 2½ lb**
1 tbsp	virgin olive oil	**1 tbsp**
2	onions, sliced	**2**
4	carrots, coarsely sliced	**4**
3	sticks celery, coarsely sliced	**3**
1	leek, trimmed and coarsely sliced	**1**
250 g	swedes, diced	**8 oz**

2	garlic cloves	**2**
2	bay leaves	**2**
	rosemary sprigs	
	parsley sprigs	
1 tbsp	fresh thyme, or 1 tsp dried	**1 tbsp**
¼ tsp	salt	**¼ tsp**
30 cl	unsalted veal or chicken stock	**½ pint**
15 cl	dry white wine	**¼ pint**

Preheat the oven to 180°C (350°F or Mark 4). Heat the oil in a large, heavy frying pan over high heat. Brown the veal—about 5 minutes. Remove the joint from the pan and set aside. Reduce the heat, add the onions, carrots, celery, leek and swedes to the oil remaining in the pan and gently cook until they glisten. Add the stock and wine, and bring to the boil. Transfer the vegetables and stock to an ovenproof casserole, place the veal on top of the vegetables and add the garlic, bay leaves, rosemary, parsley, thyme and salt. Cover the casserole with a tight-fitting lid or foil.

Braise the veal in the oven for about 2 hours, basting frequently, until tender. When cooked, transfer the veal to a hot serving dish, remove the string and cut into slices. Discard the bay leaves and herbs. Using a slotted spoon, lift two thirds of the vegetables, particularly the larger pieces, on to the serving dish. Cover and keep hot. Using a masher, mash the vegetables remaining in the stock. Bring to the boil, then pour into a hot serving jug or bowl. Serve with the veal.

Tagine of Veal with Dried Fruits and Pine-Nuts

Serves 4

Working time: about 10 minutes

Total time: about 2 hours and 15 minutes

Calories 310

Protein 29g

Cholesterol 75mg

Total fat 10g

Saturated fat 2g

Sodium 190mg

600 g	veal topside, trimmed and cut into 2 cm (¾-inch) cubes	**1¼ lb**	
½	large onion, finely chopped	**½**	
2½ tsp	ground paprika	**2½ tsp**	
1½ tsp	ground ginger	**1½ tsp**	
½ tsp	ground cinnamon	**½ tsp**	
	freshly ground black pepper		
½ tsp	salt	**½ tsp**	
125 g	dried apricots	**4 oz**	
125 g	prunes	**4 oz**	
30 g	pine-nuts	**1 oz**	
⅛ tsp	saffron threads	**⅛ tsp**	
40 cl	unsalted chicken or veal stock	**¾ pint**	
	fresh coriander sprigs for garnish		

Preheat the oven to 170°C (325°F or Mark 3). In a large bowl, mix the veal, onion, paprika, ginger, cinnamon, some pepper and the salt, until the meat is evenly coated. Add the dried fruit and pine-nuts, then transfer the mixture to the cooking pot.

Bring the stock to the boil and stir in the saffron. Pour it over the meat mixture, cover and cook in the oven for 2 hours. Serve hot, straight from the pot, garnished with coriander.

Veal, Prosciutto and Sage Sauté

Serves 4

Working (and total) time: about 15 minutes

Calories 175

Protein 23g

Cholesterol 95mg

Total fat 7g

Saturated fat 2g

Sodium 350mg

400 g	veal escalope, trimmed cut into thin strips	**14 oz**	
1 tbsp	virgin olive oil	**1 tbsp**	
45 g	thinly sliced prosciutto, trimmed, cut into thin strips	**1½ oz**	
¼ tsp	salt	**¼ tsp**	
	freshly ground black pepper		
3 tbsp	coarsely chopped fresh sage, or 2 tsp dried sage	**3 tbsp**	
4 tbsp	Marsala	**4 tbsp**	

Heat the oil in a large, non-stick frying pan over high heat. Add the strips of veal and sauté for about 1½ minutes, stirring to cook and brown the veal evenly. If the veal exudes a lot of liquid, cook until this has evaporated.

Add the prosciutto, salt and some pepper and cook the meat, stirring and tossing, for 1 minute. Add the sage and Marsala, toss for a further 30 seconds and serve immediately.

Fruit-Stuffed Veal Olives

Serves 4

Working time:
about 45
minutes

Total time:
about 1 hour
and 5 minutes

Calories
185

Protein
18g

Cholesterol
80mg

Total fat
6g

Saturated fat
1g

Sodium
200mg

4	veal escalopes, trimmed of fat and flattened	
1 tbsp	safflower oil	**1 tbsp**
About 15 cl	red grape juice	**About ¼ pint**
½ tbsp	arrowroot	**½ tbsp**
	red apples, sliced	
	seedless green grapes	

Spiced fruit stuffing		
60 g	fresh or frozen cranberries	**2 oz**
1	crisp eating apple, cored	**1**
75 g	seedless green grapes	**2½ oz**
1½ tsp	freshly grated ginger root	**1½ tsp**
½ tsp	mixed spice	**½ tsp**
½ tsp	salt	**½ tsp**
	freshly ground black pepper	

First make the stuffing. Put the cranberries, apple quarters, grapes and ginger in a food processor and blend until quite fine. Drain the fruit mixture in a fine sieve placed over a bowl to catch the juice, pressing down on the fruit to squeeze out all excess liquid; reserve the liquid. Add the mixed spice, salt and some pepper to the mixture and stir to blend. Spread one quarter of the mixture over each escalope, then roll them up, tucking in the sides. Tie each roll with string.

Heat the oil in a small, non-stick frying pan over medium-high heat. Add the veal rolls and brown them on all sides—about 5

minutes. As they are browned, transfer them to a saucepan in which they will fit comfortably. Add enough grape juice to the reserved fruit juice to make 30 cl (½ pint). Pour this over the rolls and bring to the boil. Reduce the heat, cover and simmer for 20 minutes, turning the rolls after 10 minutes.

Transfer the veal rolls to a warmed dish, slice them and keep hot. Mix the arrowroot with a little water to make a smooth paste, then stir it into the cooking liquid. Simmer, stirring constantly, until it has thickened. Pour the sauce around the veal rolls and garnish with apple slices and grapes. Serve hot.

Red-Cooked Beef

Serves 6

Working time:
about 30
minutes

Total time:
about 2 hours
and 30
minutes

Calories
270
Protein
38g
Cholesterol
75mg
Total fat
8g
Saturated fat
3g
Sodium
105mg

1 kg	beef topside, trimmed and cut into 2 cm (¾-inch) pieces	**2 lb**
4	Chinese dried mushrooms, soaked in hot water for 10 to 15 minutes	**4**
3 tbsp	low-sodium soy sauce or shoyu	**3 tbsp**
2 tbsp	dry sherry	**2 tbsp**
2 tbsp	soft brown sugar	**2 tbsp**
1 tbsp	tomato paste	**1 tbsp**
2.5 cm	fresh ginger root, crushed	**1 inch**
2	garlic cloves, crushed	**2**
½ tsp	five-spice powder	**½ tsp**
¼ litre	unsalted brown stock	**8 fl oz**
1 tbsp	safflower oil	**1 tbsp**
300 g	carrots, thinly sliced diagonally	**10 oz**

Drain the mushrooms and gently squeeze out excess moisture. Trim and slice them. Place them in a bowl with the soy sauce or shoyu, sherry, brown sugar, tomato paste, ginger, garlic, five-spice powder and stock. Stir well and set aside.

Heat the oil in a heavy fireproof casserole over high heat Add one third of the beef pieces and brown them on all sides, turning them constantly—about 5 minutes. With a slotted spoon, drain the meat, then transfer it to a plate lined with paper towels. Repeat with the remaining two batches of beef, draining each batch on fresh towels. Return all the beef to the casserole, add the mushrooms and liquid mixture and bring slowly to the boil. Reduce the heat, cover and simmer very gently for 1½ hours, turning the meat over frequently during this time and basting with the cooking liquid.

Add the carrots and continue cooking for a further 30 minutes or until the beef is tender; the carrots should be cooked but still firm. Serve hot.

Sauerbraten Stew with Crystallized Ginger

Serves 4

Working time: about 30 minutes

Total time: about 3 hours (includes marinating)

Calories 345
Protein 27g
Cholesterol 75mg
Total fat 10g
Saturated fat 3g
Sodium 390mg

1 tbsp	safflower oil	1 tbsp
500 g	lean stewing beef, trimmed of fat sliced and squared	1 lb
4 tbsp	crystallized ginger, cut into thin strips	4 tbsp
1	onion, finely chopped	1
1	carrot, finely chopped	1
1	stick celery, finely chopped	1
1	bay leaf	1

5	juniper berries, or 1 tbsp gin	5
¾ tsp	ground allspice	¾ tsp
½ tsp	salt	½ tsp
	freshly ground black pepper	
½ litre	red wine	16 fl oz
1 tbsp	red wine vinegar	1 tbsp
¼ litre	unsalted brown stock	8 fl oz
1	slice wholemeal bread, crumbled	1
2 tsp	flour	2 tsp

Heat the oil in a large, heavy frying pan over medium high heat. Add the beef squares and crystallized ginger, and cook them, turning the meat occasionally, until the beef is well browned—about 10 minutes. Transfer the beef and ginger to a large saucepan or fireproof casserole.

Reduce the heat under the frying pan to medium then add the onion, carrot, celery, bay leaf, juniper berries or gin, allspice, salt and some pepper. Cook the mixture, stirring and scraping with a wooden spoon to loosen any bits of beef, for 5 minutes. Pour in the wine and vinegar, and simmer the mixture for 1 minute. Transfer the vegetable mixture to the saucepan. Stir to combine the ingredients, then cover the pan and let the stew stand for 1 hour off the heat to marinate the beef and vegetables in the liquid. Remove the bay leaf.

Pour the stock and 17.5 cl (6 fl oz) of water into the pan. Partially cover the pan and slowly bring the liquid to a simmer. Simmer the stew, stirring occasionally, for 40 minutes. Mix the crumbled bread with the flour and stir them into the stew. Continue cooking the stew until the beef is tender—about 40 minutes.

Grilled Sirloin Steak with Peach Piccalilli

Serves 6

Working time:
about 20
minutes

Total time:
about 45
minutes

Calories
205
Protein
24g
Cholesterol
65mg
Total fat
7g
Saturated fat
3g
Sodium
185mg

850 g	sirloin steak, 2. 5 cm (1 inch) thick, trimmed of fat	**1¾ lb**	**½ tbsp**	safflower oil	**½ tbsp**
2 tsp	chopped fresh ginger root	**2 tsp**	**1 tsp**	chopped fresh ginger root	**1 tsp**
½ tsp	cayenne pepper	**½ tsp**	**⅛ tsp**	cayenne pepper	**⅛ tsp**
¼ tsp	salt	**¼ tsp**	**3 tbsp**	red wine vinegar	**3 tbsp**
	Peach piccalilli		**⅛ tsp**	salt	**⅛ tsp**
250 g	white onion	**8 oz**	**4 tbsp**	fresh orange juice	**4 tbsp**
350 g	ripe peaches	**12 oz**	**1½ tbsp**	chopped fresh coriander or parsley	**1½ tbsp**

Slice the onions in half lengthwise. Cutting with the grain, slice each half into strips about 5 mm (¼ inch) wide. Blanch the peaches in boiling water for 30 seconds, then remove them with a slotted spoon. When they are cool, peel, stone, and slice them.

Heat the oil gently in a large frying pan. Add the onion, ginger and cayenne pepper and cook until onion is translucent—7 to 10 minutes. Stir in the vinegar and salt, then cook for 1 minute more. Add the peaches and orange juice. Cook the piccalilli slowly, until the peaches are soft, but not mushy—another 12 to 15 minutes. Then remove the pan from the heat and stir in the coriander or parsley.

If you plan to barbecue the steak, light the charcoal about 30 minutes before cooking time; to grill, preheat the grill for 10 minutes. Rub the ginger and cayenne pepper into both sides of the steak, and allow it to stand at room temperature until you are ready to cook.

Cook the steak on the first side for 6 minutes, then turn it, and sprinkle it with the salt. Grill the steak on the second side for 5 to 6 minutes for medium-rare meat. Transfer the steak to a platter and let it rest for about 5 minutes before carving it into thin slices. Serve the Peach Piccalilli on the side.

Beef Salad with Carrots and Mint

850 g	rump steak in one piece, trimmed of fat	**1¾ lb**	**2 tsp**	chili paste, or ½ tsp hot red pepper flakes	**2 tsp**
4 tbsp	unsalted brown stock or unsalted chicken stock	**4 tbsp**	**2 tbsp**	chopped fresh mint, or 2 tsp dried mint	**2 tbsp**
1½ tbsp	soy sauce or shoyu	**1½ tbsp**	**250 g**	cucumber, thinly sliced	**8 oz**
4 tbsp	fresh lime juice	**4 tbsp**	**1**	sweet white onion, thinly sliced	**1**
2	garlic cloves, finely chopped	**2**	**6**	cherry tomatoes, halved	**6**
3	carrots	**3**	**250 g**	daikon radish or ordinary radishes, shredded	**8 oz**
2 tsp	sugar	**2 tsp**	**2 tbsp**	safflower oil	**2 tbsp**
	freshly ground black pepper				

Set the steak in a baking dish. Combine the stock, soy sauce, 2 tbsps of the lime juice, the garlic, sugar, some black pepper, the chili paste or red pepper flakes, and half of the mint. Pour this mixture over the steak and let it marinate at room temperature for 2 hours

Cut several shallow lengthwise grooves in each carrot. Slice them and place the resulting flowers in a large bowl. Add the cucumber, onion, tomatoes and radish to the bowl.

Remove the steak from the marinade and pat it dry. Strain the marinade into a small saucepan and bring it to the boil. Remove from the heat, whisk in the oil and the remaining 2 tbsps of lime juice, and pour the dressing over the vegetables Add the rest of the mint and toss well. Set the vegetables aside.

Grill the steak until it is medium rare—5 to 7 minutes per side. Transfer to a cutting board and leave for 10 minutes before thinly slicing.

Using a slotted spoon, transfer the vegetables to a serving dish. Arrange the steak slices on top of the vegetables; pour the dressing left in the bowl over all, and serve at once.

Barbecued Steaks with Glazed Shallots and Mushrooms

Serves 4

Working time: about 20 minutes

Total time: about 40 minutes

Calories 290

Protein 26g

Cholesterol 60mg

Total fat 9g

Saturated fat 3g

Sodium 210mg

4	entrecôte or rump steaks, trimmed	4
2 tsp	safflower oil	2 tsp
250 g	mushrooms, wiped clean	8 oz
250 g	shallots, peeled	8 oz
2 tbsp	honey	2 tbsp
1 tsp	chopped fresh tarragon, or $\frac{1}{2}$ tsp dried tarragon	1 tsp
12.5 cl	Madeira or port	4 fl oz
12.5 cl	unsalted brown or chicken stock	4 fl oz
2 tsp	cornflour, mixed with 1 tbsp of the stock	2 tsp
$\frac{1}{4}$ tsp	salt	$\frac{1}{4}$ tsp
	freshly ground black pepper	

Light the charcoal about 30 minutes before cooking time. To grill, preheat for 10 minutes.

Heat the oil in a frying pan over medium heat; add the mushrooms and saute until they are lightly browned—about 4 minutes. Using a slotted spoon, transfer the mushrooms to a bowl. Pour $\frac{1}{4}$ litre (8 fl oz) of water into the pan and add the shallots, honey and tarragon. Partially cover the pan; bring to a simmer and cook the mixture until the shallots are translucent and only 4 tablespoons of liquid remains—8 to 10 minutes.

Return the mushrooms to the pan and toss them with the shallots and the liquid until all are coated with a syrupy glaze—about 2 minutes longer. Keep the glazed shallots and mushrooms warm

In a small saucepan, reduce the Madeira or port by half over medium-high heat. Add the stock and bring the mixture to a simmer Whisk in the cornflour mixture. Cook the sauce until it thickens, and add $\frac{1}{8}$ teaspoon of the salt and some pepper. Keep the sauce warm while you prepare the steaks.

Grill or barbecue the steaks for 3 minutes. Turn them over and season with the remaining $\frac{1}{8}$ teaspoon of salt and some pepper. Cook the steaks for 3 minutes longer for medium-rare. Serve the steaks with the sauce poured on top.

Sirloin Barbecued in Garlic Smoke

<table>
<tr><td>Serves 6</td></tr>
<tr><td>Working time:
about 30
minutes</td></tr>
<tr><td>Total time:
about 45
minutes</td></tr>
</table>

Calories
220
Protein
26g
Cholesterol
75mg
Total fat
11g
Saturated fat
3g
Sodium
105mg

1 kg	sirloin steak, trimmed about 4 cm (1½ inches) thick,	**2 lb**
10	unpeeled garlic cloves, crushed	**10**
	Onion-pepper relish	
2 tbsp	safflower oil	**2 tbsp**
1	small red onion, thinly sliced	**1**
1	garlic clove, finely chopped	**1**
1 tsp	finely chopped fresh ginger root	**1 tsp**

1	sweet green pepper, seeded, deribbed and julienned	**1**
2	spring onions, trimmed and thinly sliced	**2**
2 tbsp	rice vinegar or distilled white vinegar	**2 tbsp**
¼ tsp	sugar	**¼ tsp**
⅛ tsp	salt	**¼ tsp**

About 30 minutes before cooking time, light the charcoal in the barbecue. Put the crushed garlic cloves in ¼ litre (8 fl oz) of cold water and let them soak while you make the relish.

Heat the oil in a heavy or non-stick frying pan over medium heat. Add the red onion slices and cook them, stirring frequently, until they have softened without losing their colour—3 to 4 minutes. Add the chopped garlic and ginger, and cook the mixture for 30 seconds longer; transfer it to a bowl. Add the green pepper, spring onions, vinegar, sugar and salt; stir the relish and set it aside.

When the charcoal is hot, cook the steak for 7 minutes on the first side. Drain the water from the garlic cloves. Remove the steak from the barbecue and toss the soaked garlic cloves directly on to the charcoal, a garlicky smoke will curl up. Return the steak to the barbecue and cook it on the second side for 5 to 7 minutes longer for medium-rare meat.

Transfer the steak to a platter and let it rest for 5 minutes. Carve the steak into thin slices; spread the onion-pepper relish over each portion just before serving, or present the relish on the side.

Grilled Roulades with Onion Compote

Serves 4

Working time:
about 45 minutes

Total time:
about 1 hour

Calories
230
Protein
21g
Cholesterol
45mg
Total fat
5g
Saturated fat
2g
Sodium
305mg

4	pieces of rump steak (about 125 g/4 oz each), trimmed of fat	4
600 g	pearl onions, blanched in boiling water for 5 minutes, peeled	1¼ lb
75 g	sultanas	2½ oz
⅛ tsp	salt	⅛ tsp
1 tsp	red wine vinegar	1 tsp
4 tbsp	grainy mustard	4 tbsp
4 tbsp	finely chopped fresh parsley	4 tbsp
	freshly ground black pepper	

Put the onions, sultanas, salt, vinegar and ¼ litre (8 fl oz) of water into a heavy saucepan. Bring the liquid to the boil, then reduce the heat, and simmer the mixture until the onions are golden-brown and the liquid has evaporated—15 to 20 minutes.

If you plan to barbecue the roulades, light the charcoal about 30 minutes before cooking time. To grill, preheat for about 10 minutes.

While the onion compote is reducing, butterfly and pound the steaks as shown opposite. Mix the mustard, parsley and some pepper in a small bowl and spread this mixture over the meat. Roll each steak into a loose bundle; tie the roulades with butcher's string to hold them together.

When the onions finish cooking, set them aside and keep them warm.

Grill or barbecue the beef rolls for a total of 8 minutes, turning them every 2 minutes. Transfer the rolls to a platter; serve the onion compote alongside.

Grilled Beef and Fresh Salsa in Flour Tortillas

Serves 4		Calories 375
Working (and total) time: about 1 hour		Protein 27g
		Cholesterol 60mg
		Total fat 10g
		Saturated fat 2g
		Sodium 185mg

500 g	rump steak, trimmed of fat	**1 lb**
2 tbsp	fresh lime juice	**2 tbsp**
2 tbsp	tequila or gin	**2 tbsp**
½ tsp	chili powder	**½ tsp**
½ tsp	dried oregano	**½ tsp**
¼ tsp	ground cumin	**¼ tsp**
	freshly ground black pepper	
8	spring onions, green tops, trimmed to 7.5 cm (3 inches) in length	**8**
8	large flour tortillas	**8**
110 g	cos lettuce, shredded	**4 oz**

	Salsa	
500 g	ripe tomatoes, skinned seeded and chopped	**1 lb**
1	sweet green pepper, seeded, deribbed and finely diced	**1**
1	small onion, finely chopped	**1**
1 to 3	fresh green chili peppers, seeded and finely chopped	**1 to 3**
2 tbsp	fresh lime juice	**2 tbsp**
2 tbsp	chopped fresh coriander	**2 tbsp**
¼ tsp	salt	**¼ tsp**

Slice steak against the grain into 1 cm (½ inch) wide strips. In a large, shallow dish, combine the lime juice, tequila or gin, chili powder, oregano, cumin and black pepper. Add the steak strips and the spring onions, and toss them well. Let the steak marinate at room temperature for 20 minutes.

Combine the salsa ingredients in a bowl, let stand for 15 minutes to blend the flavours

If you plan to barbecue the meat, light the charcoal about 30 minutes before cooking time; to grill, preheat for about 10 minutes.

Stack the tortillas and wrap them in foil. Warm them in at 180°C (350°F or Mark 4) for 10 minutes. Meanwhile, cook the steak strips in the centre of the grill or barbecue with the spring onions at the side, for 1 minute per side; the steak should be medium rare and the spring onions lightly charred. Cut the steak strips into pieces about 2.5 cm (1 inch) long.

To serve, place the steak pieces and their juices on the tortillas. Add some lettuce and a spring onion, then spoon some of the salsa over the top. Roll up the tortillas and serve at once.

Barbecued Veal with Spicy Orange Sauce

Serves 8

Working time about 1 hour

Total time: about 3 hours (includes marinating)

Calories 230

Protein 22g

Cholesterol 90mg

Total fat 10g

Saturated fat 3g

Sodium 160mg

1 kg	veal rump in one piece, trimmed	**2 lb**
1 tsp	allspice	**1 tsp**
1 tsp	juniper berries	**1 tsp**
2 tbsp	virgin olive oil	**2 tbsp**
¼ tsp	salt	**¼ tsp**
	freshly ground black pepper	
2	oranges, finely grated rind only	**2**
	Spicy orange sauce	
¼ litre	fresh orange juice	**8 fl oz**

4 tbsp	clear honey	**4 tbsp**
2 tbsp	red wine vinegar	**2 tbsp**
2	garlic cloves crushed	**2**
400 g	canned tomatoes, drained and sieved	**14 oz**
1 tbsp	Grand Marnier	**1 tbsp**
½ tsp	paprika	**½ tsp**
	Tabasco sauce	
¼ tsp	salt	**¼ tsp**
	freshly ground black pepper	

To prepare the marinade, crush the allspice and juniper berries together with a pestle and mortar, then blend in the oil, salt, some pepper and the grated orange rind.

Place the joint in a shallow dish, pour on the marinade and coat well. Cover and marinate at room temperature for 2 to 3 hours.

To prepare the sauce, put the orange juice, honey, wine vinegar, garlic, tomatoes and Grand Marnier in a heavy-bottomed saucepan. Add the paprika, a few drops of Tabasco sauce, the salt and some pepper. Bring to the boil, then lower the heat and simmer very

gently for 45 minutes to 1 hour, until the sauce is reduced and thickened.

Light the charcoal in the barbecue about 30 minutes before cooking time. Skewer the veal into a neat shape using one or two large skewers. Cook on a rack over hot, but not fierce, coals, turning frequently until cooked through but still slightly pink inside—35 to 45 minutes—taking care that the veal does not burn.

To serve, carefully slide the veal off the skewers on to a cutting board then cut into thin slices. Serve with the Spicy orange sauce.

Roast Loin and Sweetcorn Watercress Pilaff

Serves 8

Working time:
about 1 hour

Total time:
about 2 hours
and 15
minutes

Calories
275
Protein
30g
Cholesterol
110mg
Total fat
14g
Saturated fat
5g
Sodium
220mg

1 kg	boned loin of veal	2 lb	60 g	watercress leaves, chopped	2 oz
2 tsp	safflower oil	2 tsp	125 g	cooked brown rice	4 oz
1	onion, finely chopped	1	½ tsp	salt	½ tsp
1	stick celery, finely chopped	1		freshly ground black pepper	
2 tbsp	semi-skimmed milk	2 tbsp	4 tbsp	medium sherry	4 tbsp
300 g	sweetcorn kernels	10 oz			

Trim excess fat from the veal, being careful not to cut the membranes that hold it together. Open out the joint on a work surface.

Preheat the oven to 180°C (350°F or Mark 4). Gently heat the oil in a small frying pan. Add the onion and celery and cook until softened—about 5 minutes, then put in a bowl.

Put the milk in a food processor and add 30 g (1 oz) rice. Blend them to a smooth paste, then turn the paste into a bowl.

Add the sweetcorn kernels and watercress to the onion and celery. Season and mix together. Mix a quarter of this with the rice paste, then spread the paste over the veal. Roll it up and tie with string, then place it in a roasting bag and sit it in a roasting pan.

Add the remaining rice to the rest of the sweetcorn mixture and spoon it into the roasting bag round the joint. Close the end of the bag with a plastic tie, and cut several slits. Roast for 1¼ to 1½ hours; test if the veal is cooked by piercing it through one of the slits in the bag. The juices that run out of the meat should be only faintly pink, or clear.

Cut open the top of the roasting bag and lift the joint on to a carving dish. Transfer the sweetcorn-watercress pilaff to the dish, draining well and arranging it round the joint. Cover and set aside for 10 minutes.

Meanwhile, strain the cooking juices left in the bag into a small saucepan. Add the sherry, bring to the boil and boil for 1 minute.

Carve the veal into thick slices on the bed of pilaff, and serve with the sherried juices.

Beef Stew with Stout

Serves 6

Working time;
about 40
minutes

Total time:
about 2 hours
and 40
minutes

Calories
260

Protein
27g

Cholesterol
75mg

Total fat
10g

Saturated fat
3g

Sodium
265mg

750 g	stewing beef, cubed	1½ lb	¼ litre	unsalted brown or	16 fl oz
250 g	button mushrooms, halved	8 oz		chicken stock	
1½ tbsp	safflower oil	1½ tbsp	35 cl	stout or dark beer	35 cl
2 tbsp	dark brown sugar	2 tbsp	½ tsp	salt	½ tsp
125 g	button mushrooms, wiped clean and sliced	4 oz	1	large onion, chopped freshly ground black pepper	1

Heat 1 tablespoon of the safflower oil in a large, heavy frying-pan over medium-high heat. Add the beef cubes and sauté them, turning frequently, until they are browned all over—about 8 minutes. Using a slotted spoon, transfer the beef to a heavy-bottomed saucepan.

Add the remaining oil to the frying-pan along with the onion, mushrooms and brown sugar. Sauté the mixture, stirring frequently, until the mushrooms begin to brown and their liquid has evaporated—about ten minutes. Transfer the onion-mushroom mixture to the saucepan, then add the stock, the stout or dark beer, the salt and some pepper.

Reduce the heat to very low, cover the saucepan, and gently simmer the stew until the beef is tender—1½ to 2 hours.

South-East Asian Beef Noodles

Serves 4

Working (and total) time: about 45 minutes

Calories 420

Protein 33g

Cholesterol 70mg

Total fat 13g

Saturated fat 3g

Sodium 260mg

600 g	rump steak, trimmed thinly sliced	**1¼ lb**
1 tbsp	soy sauce or shoyu	**1 tbsp**
2 tbsp	dry sherry or dry white wine	**2 tbsp**
2 tbsp	sugar	**2 tbsp**
	freshly ground black pepper	
1½ tbsp	cornflour	**1½ tbsp**
175 g	Asian wheat noodles	**6 oz**
4 tsp	safflower oil	**4 tsp**
1	small onion sliced lengthwise	**1**

1	carrot, diagonally sliced	**1**
250 g	broccoli stems, diagonally sliced	**8 oz**
½	sweet red pepper, cut in strips	**½**
2 tsp	ginger root	**2 tsp**
4	garlic cloves, finely chopped	**4**
¼ litre	unsalted brown or chicken stock	**8 fl oz**
½ tbsp	sweet chili sauce	**½ tbsp**
1 tbsp	fresh lemon juice	**1 tbsp**
1 tbsp	hoisin sauce	**1 tbsp**

Combine the beef, soy sauce, sherry or wine, 1 tbsp sugar, some pepper and ½tblsp cornflour. Set the mixture aside

Cook the noodles in 3 litres (5 pints) of boiling water until they are *al dente*. Drain and rinse the pasta, cover and keep warm.

Heat 2 tsps of oil in a frying pan or wok over high heat. Add the onion slices and stir-fry for 1 minute. Mix in the sweet red pepper and stir-fry for 2 minutes. Mound the vegetables on the pasta, cover, and keep warm.

Heat the remaining oil in the pan or wok over high heat. Add the ginger and garlic,

and stir until the ginger is brown—about 2 minutes. Add the beef and marinade, and stir-fry until no traces of pink remain—1 to 2 minutes. Spoon the mixture on to the centre of the vegetables and keep the platter warm.

Pour the stock into the pan and bring to the boil. Mix the remaining cornflour with 2 tbsps of water in a bowl. Stir into the stock the cornflour mixture, chili sauce or red-pepper-flake mixture, the remaining sugar, lemon juice, and hoisin sauce. Simmer until it thickens—about 1 minute. Pour the sauce over the beef and serve it immediately.

Steak Braised in Spicy Vinegar Sauce

Serves 4

Working time: about 15 minutes

Total time: about 4 hours 15minutes (includes marinating)

Calories 235
Protein 28g
Cholesterol 80mg
Total fat 11g
Saturated fat 3g
Sodium 245mg

600 g	sirloin steak, trimmed and cut into four pieces	**1¼ lb**
1	garlic clove, finely chopped	**1**
1 tbsp	chopped fresh oregano, or 1 tsp dried oregano	**1 tbsp**
	hot red pepper flakes	
4 tbsp	balsamic vinegar	**4 tbsp**
1 tbsp	safflower oil	**1 tbsp**
¼ tsp	salt	**¼ tsp**
	freshly ground black pepper	
400 g	canned whole tomatoes, with their juice	**14 oz**
2 tbsp	freshly grated Parmesan cheese	**2**
tbsp	parsley sprigs	

Put the pieces of meat into a shallow, non-reactive dish and add the garlic, oregano, a pinch of red pepper flakes and the vinegar. Let the meat marinate for 3 hours in the refrigerator. Drain the meat and pat the pieces dry, reserving the marinade.

Heat the oil in a large, heavy, fireproof casserole over medium-high heat. Sear the meat on both sides, then season it with the salt and some black pepper. Puree the tomatoes in a food processor or a blender and add them and the reserved marinade to the casserole. Cover it and simmer the meat in the sauce for 30 minutes. Turn the meat, replace the cover, and continue braising the pieces until they are tender—about 30 to 45 minutes.

Transfer the beef to a heated platter and spoon the sauce over it. Serve the dish topped with the grated cheese and garnished with parsley sprigs.

Persian Veal and Bean Stew with Parsley

Serves 4

Working time: about 45 minutes

Total time: about 10 hours and 15 minutes (includes soaking)

Calories 415
Protein 35g
Cholesterol 105mg
Total fat 15g
Saturated fat 3g
Sodium 400mg

350 g	topside of veal or top rump, trimmed and minced	**12 oz**
125 g	dried chick-peas, soaked for 8 hours, drained	**4 oz**
125 g	dried red kidney beans, soaked for 8 hours, drained	**4 oz**
2 tbsp	safflower oil	**2 tbsp**
1	large onion, chopped	**1**
1	garlic clove, finely chopped	**1**
2	sticks celery, sliced	**2**
90 g	parsley, stems removed, chopped	**3 oz**
4 tbsp	lemon juice	**4 tbsp**
45 cl	unsalted veal or chicken stock	**¾ pint**
1 tsp	ground allspice	**1 tsp**
30 g	fresh wholemeal breadcrumbs	**1 oz**
½ tsp	salt	**½ tsp**
	freshly ground black pepper	
½	egg, beaten	**½**

Put the chick-peas and kidney beans in separate saucepans and cover with fresh water. Bring to the boil and boil for 10 minutes Drain and set aside.

Heat 1 tbsp of oil in a 30 cm (12 inch) diameter, shallow casserole. Add the onion, garlic, celery and 60 g (2 oz) parsley. Cover and cook gently for about 10 minutes or until the vegetables are softened. Add the chickpeas, lemon juice, half the stock and the allspice and stir. Bring to the boil, cover again and simmer for 30 minutes. Stir in the kidney beans with half the remaining stock. Cover again and simmer for 30 minutes.

Meanwhile, combine the veal, breadcrumbs, remaining parsley, half the salt and some pepper in a bowl. Mix together and add enough egg to bind. Divide into 12 equal portions and shape into balls. Heat the remaining oil in a frying pan over medium-high heat. Add the meatballs and brown on all sides, turning them and shaking the pan so that they colour evenly—about 5 minutes.

Add the meatballs to the bean stew. Add the remaining salt and some pepper. Simmer, covered, for a further 1 hour or until the beans are tender, stirring occasionally and adding a little extra stock if necessary.

Grilled Entrecote Steaks with Fennel Scented Vegetables

Serves 8

Working time about 20 minutes

Total time about 40 minutes

Calories
235
Protein
26g
Cholesterol
65mg
Total fat
10g
Saturated fat
39g
Sodium
200mg

4	entrecôte steaks, trimmed (about 300 g/10 oz each)	**4**
2 tbsp	olive oil	**2 tbsp**
1½ tsp	fennel seeds, lightly crushed	**1½ tsp**
3	garlic cloves, thinly sliced	**3**
500 g	aubergine, diced	**1 lb**
175 g	onion, chopped	**6 oz**
2 tbsp	fresh lemon juice	**2 tbsp**
750 g ·	ripe tomatoes, skinned, seeded and diced	**1½ lb**
½ tsp	salt	**½ tsp**
	freshly ground black pepper	

If you plan to barbecue the steaks, light the charcoal about 30 minutes before cooking time; to grill, preheat for about 10 minutes.

In the meantime, heat the olive oil in a large, heavy frying pan over high heat. When the oil is hot, add the fennel seeds and garlic, and cook them for 30 seconds, stirring constantly. Add the aubergine, onion and lemon juice and cook the vegetables for 5 minutes, stirring frequently. Next, add the tomatoes, ¼ teaspoon of salt and a generous grinding of pepper to the pan. Cook the

vegetable mixture for 3 to 4 minutes longer, stirring continuously. Cover the pan and set the mixture aside while you finish the dish.

Grill or barbecue the steaks for 3 to 4 minutes. Turn the steaks and sprinkle with the remaining ¼ teaspoon of salt and some pepper. Cook the steaks for an additional 3 to 4 minutes for medium-rare meat. Let them stand for 5 minutes before thinly slicing them against the grain. Divide the meat and vegetables among eight dinner plates and serve at once.

Steaks Creole

Serves 4

Working time:
about 45
minutes

Total time:
about 5 hours
(includes
marinating)

Calories
320
Protein
29g
Cholesterol
60mg
Total fat
11g
Saturated fat
3g
Sodium
120mg

500 g	sirloin or entrecôte steaks, trimmed of fat, cut into four 2 cm (¾ inch) thick pieces	**1 lb**
350 g	fresh pineapple, peeled, skinned and sliced crosswise	**12 oz**
350 g	watermelon, peeled and sliced	**12 oz**
1	papaya, peeled, halved, seeded and sliced	**1**
1	mango, peeled, stoned and sliced	**1**
1 tbsp	virgin olive oil	**1 tbsp**

2 tbsp	lime juice	**2 tbsp**
2 tsp	chopped fresh mint	**2 tsp**
⅛ tsp	salt	**⅛ tsp**
	Rum marinade	
2 tbsp	dark rum	**2 tbsp**
½ tsp	virgin olive oil	**½ tsp**
2	garlic cloves, crushed	**2**
12	whole allspice berries, crushed	**12**
1 tsp	cayenne pepper	**1 tsp**
	freshly ground black pepper	

To make the marinade, mix together the rum, oil, garlic, allspice, cayenne pepper and some black pepper. Put the beef in a shallow dish and brush the marinade over both sides of each steak. Cover loosely and leave to marinate in a cold place or the refrigerator for at least 4 hours, preferably overnight.

Before cooking, let the steaks stand at room temperature for 30 minutes. Mean-while, arrange the sliced fruit on individual plates. Whisk together the oil, lime juice, mint and salt, and set aside.

Place the steaks in a heavy, non-stick frying pan over high heat. Cook for 4 minutes on each side for rare steaks, longer if you prefer them well done. Arrange the steaks on the plates with the fruit. Dribble the dressing over the fruit or serve it separately. Serve at once.

Veal Chops with Artichokes

Serves 4		Calories 280
Working time about 45 minutes		Protein 24g
Total time: about 2 hours		Cholesterol 120mg
		Total fat 17g
		Saturated fat 6g
		Sodium 315mg

4	veal loin chops, trimmed (about 250 g/8 oz each)	4
4 tbsp	lemon juice	4 tbsp
4	globe artichokes,	4
1 tbsp	safflower oil	1 tbsp
4 tbsp	dry sherry	4 tbsp
1½ tbsp	chopped fresh tarragon	1½ tbsp
½ tsp	salt	½ tsp
	freshly ground black pepper	
2 tbsp	double cream	2 tbsp

Cut the stems off the artichokes close to the base and place them bottom down in 2 litres (3½ pints) of boiling water. Simmer for about 30 minutes. To test if they are cooked, a leaf gently tugged should pull free. Drain by putting them upside down in a colander.

Preheat the oven to 180°C (350°F or Mark 4).

When cool enough to handle, pull off the leaves until you reach the hairy choke; reserve the leaves and discard the choke, then trim the artichoke bottoms into neat rounds, reserving the trimmings. Cut the bottoms into 5 mm (¼ inch) cubes.

Heat the oil in a large, frying pan over high heat. Add the chops and brown them for 1 to 2 minutes. Transfer them to a sheet of foil placed over a baking sheet. Pile the diced artichoke bottoms on the chops, then sprinkle over the sherry, two thirds of the tarragon, the salt and some pepper. Wrap the foil round the chops and seal tightly. Put them in the oven and bake for 30 minutes.

Meanwhile, using a table knife, scrape off the bottom of each artichoke leaf and put it in a food processor with the reserved trimmings.

Carefully transfer the chops to a serving platter and keep hot. To make the sauce, pour the cooking juices from the foil into the food processor and blend the artichoke mixture. Pass the mixture through a fine sieve into a small saucepan and add the cream. Bring to the boil and boil for 1 minute. Spoon the sauce over the chops, sprinkle with the remaining tarragon, and serve immediately.

Terrine of Pigeon and Veal

Serves 20

Working time: about 25 minutes

Total time: about 14 hours (includes marinating and chilling)

Calories 95
Protein 14g
Cholesterol 40mg
Total fat 3g
Saturated fat 1g
Sodium 130mg

4	pigeon breasts, skinned	4
6 tbsp	dry Madeira	6 tbsp
1 tbsp	balsamic vinegar, or 2 tsp red wine vinegar mixed with ¼ tsp honey	1 tbsp
1 kg	minced veal	2 lb
60 g	fine fresh white breadcrumbs	2 oz
1 tbsp	finely chopped parsley	1 tbsp
1 tbsp	juniper berries	1 tbsp
2 tsp	salt	2 tsp
	freshly ground black pepper	
4	egg whites	4

Place the pigeon breasts in a shallow dish and pour on 4 tablespoons of the Madeira and the balsamic vinegar. Cover and leave the to marinate overnight in the refrigerator.

Preheat the oven to 180°C (350°F or Mark 4). Combine the veal, breadcrumbs, parsley and remaining Madeira in a bowl. Reserving a few juniper berries for garnish, crush the remainder and add them to the veal mixture. Season with salt and some black pepper. Whisk the egg whites until they stand in soft peaks, then stir them into the veal mixture.

Place about a third of the veal mixture in a 1.5 litre (2½ pint) oval terrine and press it down evenly in the bottom of the dish. Lay two of the pigeon breasts on top of the veal

mixture. Spoon another third of the mixture over the pigeon, spreading it in an even layer. Lay the remaining pigeon breasts in the terrine and top them with a final layer of veal. Pour remaining marinade over the terrine.

Place the bay leaves and the reserved juniper berries on top of the veal mixture. Cover the terrine closely with foil and stand the dish in a large roasting pan. Pour in boiling water to come two thirds of the way up the side of the terrine. Bake until a skewer inserted into the middle of the terrine feels hot to the touch when withdrawn—about 2 hours. Leave the terrine to cool—about 1 hour—then chill it in the refrigerator for at least 2 hours, or overnight, before serving.

Useful weights and measures

Weight Equivalents

Avoirdupois   *Metric*
1 ounce   =   28.35 grams
1 pound   =   254.6 grams
2.3 pounds   =   1 kilogram

Liquid Measurements

$^1/_4$ pint   = $1^1/_2$ decilitres
$^1/_2$ pint   = $^1/_4$ litre
scant 1 pint   = $^1/_2$ litre
$1^3/_4$ pints   =   1 litre
1 gallon   =   4.5 litres

Liquid Measures

1 pint	= 20 fl oz	= 32 tablespoons
$^1/_2$ pint	= 10 fl oz	= 16 tablespoons
$^1/_4$ pint	= 5 fl oz	= 8 tablespoons
$^1/_8$ pint	= $2^1/_2$ fl oz	= 4 tablespoons
$^1/_{16}$ pint	= $1^1/_4$ fl oz	= 2 tablespoons

Solid Measures

1 oz almonds, ground = $3^3/_4$ level tablespoons
1 oz breadcrumbs fresh = 7 level tablespoons
1 oz butter, lard = 2 level tablespoons
1 oz cheese, grated = $3^1/_2$ level tablespoons
1 oz cocoa = $2^3/_4$ level tablespoons
1 oz desiccated coconut = $4^1/_2$ tablespoons
1 oz cornflour = $2^1/_2$ tablespoons
1 oz custard powder = $2^1/_2$ tablespoons
1 oz curry powder and spices = 5 tablespoons
1 oz flour = 2 level tablespoons
1 oz rice, uncooked = $1^1/_2$ tablespoons
1 oz sugar, caster and granulated = 2 tablespoons
1 oz icing sugar = $2^1/_2$ tablespoons
1 oz yeast, granulated = 1 level tablespoon

American Measures

16 fl oz   =1 American pint
8 fl oz   =1 American standard cup
0.50 fl oz   =1 American tablespoon
(*slightly smaller than British Standards Institute tablespoon*)
0.16 fl oz   =1 American teaspoon

Australian Cup Measures
(*Using the 8-liquid-ounce cup measure*)

1 cup flour	4 oz
1 cup sugar (crystal or caster)	8 oz
1 cup icing sugar (free from lumps)	5 oz
1 cup shortening (butter, margarine)	8 oz
1 cup brown sugar (lightly packed)	4 oz
1 cup soft breadcrumbs	2 oz
1 cup dry breadcrumbs	3 oz
1 cup rice (uncooked)	6 oz
1 cup rice (cooked)	5 oz
1 cup mixed fruit	4 oz
1 cup grated cheese	4 oz
1 cup nuts (chopped)	4 oz
1 cup coconut	$2^1/_2$ oz

Australian Spoon Measures

	level tablespoon
1 oz flour	2
1 oz sugar	$1^1/_2$
1 oz icing sugar	2
1 oz shortening	1
1 oz honey	1
1 oz gelatine	2
1 oz cocoa	3
1 oz cornflour	$2^1/_2$
1 oz custard powder	$2^1/_2$

Australian Liquid Measures
(*Using 8-liquid-ounce cup*)

1 cup liquid	8 oz
$2^1/_2$ cups liquid	20 oz (1 pint)
2 tablespoons liquid	1 oz
1 gill liquid	5 oz ($^1/_4$ pint)